From Africa

to AMERICA

From Africa
to AMERICA
THE JOURNEY OF A LOST BOY OF SUDAN

JOSEPH AKOL MAKEER

The author lives
in Fargo and
recently graduated
from NDSU.

TATE PUBLISHING *& Enterprises*

Published by Tate Publishing & Enterprises, LLC
127 E. Trade Center Terrace | Mustang, Oklahoma 73064 USA
1.888.361.9473 | www.tatepublishing.com

Tate Publishing is committed to excellence in the publishing industry. The company reflects the philosophy established by the founders, based on Psalm 68:11,
"The Lord gave the word and great was the company of those who published it."

Book design copyright © 2007 by Tate Publishing, LLC. All rights reserved.
Cover design by Kellie Southerland
Interior design by Isaiah R. McKee

Published in the United States of America

ISBN: 978-1-60462-160-0
1. Christian Nonfiction:Autobiography   2. Africa

07.11.05

DEDICATION

This work is dedicated to Adual Aguer Bior and to Makeer and Deng, whose caring support made this book possible, and to the memory of my parents, Makeer Galuak Akol and Nyandeng Mier Deng, who passed on a love of family and hard work and a respect for education.

ACKNOWLEDGMENTS

Thanks to Mary Pull, English instructor and Director of the Center for Writers at North Dakota State University, for correcting my manuscript and for introducing me to the great people of Eagle Valley Evangelical Free Church of Christine, North Dakota.

Thanks to all the members of the Makeer family: Agot, Achol, Dau Tor, Akon, Leek Geu, Jacob, Alakiir Mabil, Abuk, Anyang Reng, Ajueny, Mathiang Bul, Aja, Amer, Agot, Akon, Apat Dau, Nyantet Elijah, Nyandeng Anyang, Deng Leek, Gai Dau, Beti Elijah, Abak Anyang, Nyandeng Elijah, Ayen Leek, Adau Dau, Nyapac Anyang, Nyandeng Elijah, Nyanacie Elijah, Makeer Leek, Makeer Elijah, Akon Anyang, Nyandeng Leek, Duotdit Dau, Akuol Anyang, Ajok Mathiang, and Nyandeng Dau. I love you. May God Almighty keep you in His love, grace, blessing, and supervision wherever you go and in whatever you do. As Makeer's family grows, may you keep Makeer Galuak Akol, Nyandeng Mier Deng, and Elijah Mapiou Choul in your prayers for laying the foundation of this wonderful family.

Thanks also to my dearest friends: Peter Bul Deng, Mawai Dut Jang, Marko Wel Aleu, Leek Jogaak Deng, Kuol Madhier Anyang, Ayuel Aleer Deng, Deng Maruon Mier, Akoy Lual Machot, Malual Kuai Awuol, and Emanuel Elijah Mapiou.

Thanks to the Lost Boys and citizens of southern Sudan for giving me this chance to be one of the voices of our time.

Thanks to Bob Rosenvold for all he has done for me and my family.

Thanks to my much-loved college, North Dakota State University (NDSU), and to President Joseph Chapman, staff members, students, and Bison fans for hosting the Lost Boys of Fargo-Moorhead.

Thanks to Dr. Kevin Brooks and Dr. Betsy Birmingham of the NDSU English Department for being helpful throughout my learning at NDSU.

Thanks to my advisor, Dr. T.D. McDonald of NDSU, for providing detailed guidance, brilliant lectures, and encouragement throughout the course of my studies.

Special thanks to John Marks of Trollwood Art School, Dr. Kevin Brooks of North Dakota State University, Debra Dawson (writer), Dayna Delval of Minnesota State University-Moorehead, Greg Carlson of Concordia College, and J.J Gordon and Matt McGregor of KVLY-TV 11 for their joined efforts in helping me make a movie about my siblings and me. Thanks to Patrick Brown (writer, advertising, & marketing), Adrian Dawson (webdesigner), and Mike Berreth (webdesigner).

TABLE OF CONTENTS

FOREWORD

I met Akol Makeer in the fall of 2004 when he came to the Center for Writers at North Dakota State University when he was writing a paper for a class. A few months later, he returned with twenty pages of text and asked me to help him edit his story for publication. As I read his draft, I thought he must have exaggerated his experiences because I had never met anyone who had lived through so much turmoil. After conducting some background research, I realized that he was telling the truth, and I knew that his story needed to be told.

Why do I want others to read Akol's story? The answer is simple: Just hearing sound-bites on the evening news is not enough; to be truly sensitized to the suffering of millions of people who have been persecuted in southern Sudan and elsewhere, we must see the horrors of genocide through the eyes of those who have survived, such as the Lost Boys of Sudan. As I worked closely with Akol on this book, I sensed the hatred and violence that tore his life and his country apart: I watched as he grew up in a traditional African culture without machinery and technology; as he saw warplanes drop bombs on helpless villagers; as he saw helpless men, women, and children tortured and killed by radical militia; as he said tearful good-byes to loved ones and walked barefoot over hot, dusty deserts and through sharp, thorny bushes; as he experienced corruption and greed in U.N. refugee camps; as he bribed officials to help his three younger siblings; and as he immigrated to a distant country with a cold climate, strange food, and stark white faces who speak a foreign language. Akol's story touched me deeply, and I now have a better understanding of the events I see reported in the media because I know how similar horrors played out in the life of a little boy who grew into manhood only through the grace of God and the help of people who cared enough to offer him a new beginning.

Thus, I hope and pray that the experiences in this book will not simply astound readers but also motivate them to support organizations that bring food and shelter to dangerous lands, to encourage our government to promote democracy in oppressed countries, and to work in their own neighborhoods and communities to make this world a better place. America has long stood for freedom, equality, and justice, but we cannot sit back and simply mind our own business. All of us must get involved to make our "shining city on a hill" a beacon of hope to people in Africa, Asia, the Middle East, and everywhere that the darkness of men's hearts inflicts cruelty on the innocent.

Mary Pull, North Dakota State University

INTRODUCTION

In Sudan in the 1980s, the Muslim government in the north restricted access to public services to only the followers of Islam. Christians in the south were not able go to school, to work at higher-paying jobs, or to receive medical treatment and other privileges. Only a few black southerners were given privileges if they agreed to help the government control the people. On May 16, 1987, angry youths from southern Sudan began to rebel against the government to gain their rights as citizens, but those who dared to speak out were killed by government troops, and their peaceful demonstrations were bombed by the warplanes of the national army. As rebel forces banded together to fight back, their uprising only fueled the racism and hatred of the Islamic government, so it began systematic bombings of villages to root out the rebels.

The graphic photos that have appeared in American media reports tell only a small part of the horrendous human rights violations that have been committed against innocent Christian Sudanese. Muslim tormentors viewed Christians as legitimate targets for lynching because there were no criminal penalties for violent acts against non-Muslims. Thousands of innocent victims were horrendously beaten, shot, drowned, and bombed by government troops. Hundreds were mutilated beyond recognition and left in the Sudanese desert about thirty kilometers from Malakal. Even though a peace treaty has been signed in southern Sudan, two decades of genocide have left more than 2 million dead and 5 million displaced as refugees to the neighboring countries of Ethiopia, Kenya, and Uganda. Some of these refugees now known as the Lost Boys of Sudan have sought asylum in the United States. I was only ten years old when this nightmare began. This is my story.

JOURNEY 1: FROM PEACEFUL VILLAGE TO WAR ZONE

Without a hospital, a clinic, or even a midwife, my mother gave birth to me in a grass hut in Duk Payuel in southern Sudan. Neither of my parents knew the day or month of my birth because they did not have a calendar. In our third-world existence, we only knew months by the appearance of the new moon, and we referred to the years by their worst natural disasters such as earthquakes or floods. At that time, the few Christians in the area counted the days of the week so they could know when to hold Sunday religious services, but those who worshipped our village god, Deng-Pajerbe, did not need to mark the weeks. Years later, when I arrived in the part of the world that needed the date of my birth, I randomly chose a day and a month, but I was able to determine that I must have been born in 1977 because my parents had told me that I was six years old when the war broke out in 1983.

Ours was a "typical small town" in the upper-Nile region. We called it a town for several reasons: a few small "shops" sold secondhand clothes and food staples such as salt and sorghum; the local chiefs held "court" as they gathered during the day to solve disputes between the people in the area; and our "police" were strong men paid by the chiefs to keep order and catch criminals. Our lifestyle was like all the other people in southern Sudan: We had our tribal customs and the same third-world standard of living. We lived in simple grass huts without electricity or running water, and every family practiced subsistence farming by growing maize, sorghum, sweet potatoes, and beans. Even though our climate was hot and dry, the rainy season brought enough moisture for our crops, so we had enough food. Gender roles were simple: Women cooked and planted the crops; men tended the cattle. Each family built its own hut with tall grass, small trees, and mud to seal the walls. All the work was done with crude hand tools, just as it had been done by the Dinka tribe for thousands of years.

As in most cultures, class distinctions affected our relationships; hunters and fishermen were poor, so they could not socialize with people who owned large herds of cows. The land was owned by the tribes and clans, so only those with relatives in an area were allowed to move there. Along the Nile River, the tribes had borders that could not be crossed without permission from the tribal leaders. If the borders were not respected, deadly fights broke out between the tribes, but we were able to live in peace, for the most part. Until 1983, our worst enemies were the lions and hyenas in the wild and diseases such as malaria. Doctors were unknown to us—we had only our witchdoctors to "treat" our illnesses. I can remember several times when my friends, siblings, and I were taken to the witchdoctor for our eyes, for a fever, or for other illnesses because our religion was animism when I was very young.

In our polygamous culture, our families were large. All the little boys were kept away from their mothers as much as possible because the men believed that women were inferior and unable to raise boys to be wise men who would make good decisions. No one dared to praise his mother instead of his father in public because everyone would laugh at him. In fact, the worst insult someone could give a Dinka male was to call him by his mother's name.

My days were happy when I was young because my parents

made sure that I was well fed and safe from the wild animals that lived all around us. Since I was the only boy in my immediate family, my father, Makeer, kept me isolated with him even when we were not working. Fortunately, he had four wives who lived far apart, so he left me for many weeks and even months. Those times were special to me because I could enjoy the love of my mother, Nyandeng, and the friendship of my sisters. I had to be careful, though, because I did not know when my father might come home. When I laughed and joked with my sisters and mother, I always sat a distance to avoid trouble if my father should return. If I was caught with the women, my father became angry and blamed my mother for encouraging me to talk to them. He would also punish me by making me do odd jobs such as cutting trees and making pegs for tethering the cattle. I did not mind the work, but I did not like his icy stare as he watched me.

When I was four years old, I began helping my father take care of our cattle. I cannot remember how many cows we had because our herd was large. He also kept some heifers and cows hidden from everyone but his favorite son—me. We used to visit his secret places so that I could learn the locations and how to identify the animals by their colors in case he died suddenly. Such secrets were not revealed to any other friends, relatives, or even his wives—only to me. Daughters were not given inheritances, so I was his only heir at the time. I knew that I must guard our secrets well because our special bond as father and son would be broken if I betrayed his trust. My mother advised me not to annoy my father in any way because I must maintain our close relationship.

At the age of five, I was old enough to work alone. My father bought me spears to protect myself and our cattle from the wild animals when I took the cattle to graze each morning and brought them home in the evening. Those days were enjoyable because I could play with many other boys my age who also brought their cattle to graze.

After a year, though, in 1982, my father changed his mind and enrolled me in the first school to be started in our region. The teacher taught us Arabic as we sat on the ground outside under the trees. School was so expensive that my father needed to sell one cow that year to pay my fees. While I was in class, my father took the cattle to graze, but I had to find them and bring them home when school was finished.

I was really confused at that time because I could not understand what my father was trying to do. He was training me to be a nomadic cattle herder, but he was also encouraging me to get an education. I preferred to be nomadic because I wanted to be like the others in my clan when I became a man. I wanted to tattoo my face, to remove my bottom teeth, and to wear expensive ivory bracelets that cost five cows, but my father did not care what I wanted because he wanted me to go to school.

I was not interested in school because I saw no need for an education, especially since my father had not gone to school. I had never seen cars, doctors, teachers, or houses built out of wood and siding to convince me that getting an education could be better for me than taking care of cows. When I asked him why I needed to go to school, he would not answer me. Finally, after I had asked him many times, he told me that he wanted me to be "rich" after school, but he could not tell me where the "rich" would come from.

As I grew, I enjoyed the wrestling and traditional dancing between the clans in my area. In wrestling, there was no limit to the number of participants because the games were free to all. Young men who did not want to wrestle needed to have good excuses because the girls laughed at weak men and avoided them. During the dances, every young man composed songs praising other people such as their fathers, siblings, mothers, girls, and clans. The girls chose their favorite men to dance with, but they could not choose their relatives. It is a taboo belief in my tribe that your bone could break while dancing with relatives. Young men and girls used cow urine on their hair to dye it a reddish color.

To mark the end of boyhood and to enter manhood, a male had to kill a cow for the first time. Then the meat was given, not sold, to others of the same age or older than the butcher because we believed that the man who ate the meat of the cow he killed could develop a mental disorder. After that rite of passage, men could develop friendships with girls. The dry season gave many opportunities for the young people to get acquainted because all the young men and women joined together in what the Dinka tribe called "Wut"—they left their families and moved their cattle to the swampy areas along the Nile River to feed. The cattle mixed together when grazing, but the young men separated them in the evening and tethered them on small pegs at night. The only job the girls did was to milk the cows—and get to know the men.

These friendships were not intended to lead to weddings because marriages were arranged by the families. Normally, fathers arranged marriages for their children, and the father of the groom paid a dowry for the bride. A disfigured or disabled bride might cost fifteen cows, but a beautiful, healthy bride could cost fifty or more cows. A son who fell in love with a woman could ask his father to agree to the match, but the father could refuse if he did not approve of the bride or her family. If the son married the woman against his father's wishes, the son had to pay the entire dowry amount by himself.

In fact, all families needed to cultivate good reputations to ensure that good matches could be made for their sons and daughters; stories of crimes such as murder, theft, and divorce could cause problems for everyone in the family—even distant relatives. As in most cultures, social behavior must also follow certain codes to be acceptable. For example, no one could eat or drink with someone who was not a relative, even if the person extended an invitation. Likewise, grooms were forbidden to drink or eat in the homes of their future in-laws until after the wedding. These codes were learned during community dances as people sang songs to praise those who followed our customs and to condemn those who broke the "rules" of our society.

Wedding ceremonies usually took place in the spring when food was abundant and no mosquitoes would torment the guests. The exact day of the wedding was announced about seven days in advance by the groom's father. Marriages were held in the groom's home, so the groom's family prepared all the food; the bride's family simply waited until everything was ready. Because the wedding celebration could last from two to four days, the groom's family had many preparations to make.

When the wedding day came, the elders from both sides of the families met to bless the new couple in the bride's home. Most of the weddings were held at night, so the groom and his friends came to walk the bride and her friends back to the groom's house. Before the groom's family could let the new guests eat, the male relatives and friends gave gifts to all the girls. The groom had to give his new wife a valuable gift, such as a goat, as a sign that she was welcome to eat with his family. Each day of the celebration, a bull or goat was slaughtered, and the guests could feast on meat, beans, maize, and plenty of fresh fruit, such as mangoes and bananas.

Weddings were very expensive because the bride normally brought about fifty of her friends to stay with the groom's family for two weeks after the wedding. The host family had no choice but to treat its guests well by providing good food, bedding, and other needs because the girls composed songs to be sung by the whole community during the games, dancing, and wrestling. For example, the girls might praise the groom's family for owning a large farm, good huts, and many cows, or they might criticize a small farm and reveal weakness, laziness, bad behavior, and bad teeth in the family or extended relatives. During this time, the groom stayed away from his bride until all her friends returned to their homes. The mother of the bride usually met with the groom to discuss the negative and positive behaviors of her daughter so the groom could learn about his new wife.

Another huge expense for the groom's family was the dowry. During the marriage celebration, all the relatives of the groom's family gave cows to the bride's family and extended family, so the bigger the bride's family, the bigger the dowry would be. First, each of the bride's brothers chose five of the best cattle; then the mother chose twenty to twenty-five cows, and the father chose two or three. The girl's uncles could take two or three cows from the groom's uncles, and the oldest aunt took one cow from the groom's aunt. Even dead grandparents were given cows. If the bride's brothers or parents did not like the cattle, or if the groom's family felt the bride's family was demanding too much, the marriage was cancelled. If the dowry pleased both sides, the bride's family was served food and homemade beer prepared by the groom's relatives.

Traditionally, each tribe and clan in Sudan worshipped its own gods; our clan was called Palual in the Dinka tribe, and our clan god was Deng-Pajerbe. Each fall, we traveled hundreds of miles to the village of our ancestors, Pajerbe, to pay our respects and to sacrifice thirty bulls to please our god and ancestors.

Parents would often bring their children to be blessed, so I was taken in 1980 and again in 1982. Later, when we became Christians, we stopped the trips and the sacrifices.

In the mid-1970s, Episcopal missionaries moved to our area and began to talk about Jesus Christ and a new religion. A few of our women and children became Christians and began attending Sunday church services, but most people were resistant because they truly believed that their clan gods were all powerful. Christianity did not appeal to the men because they feared losing their positions in the clan and because they made money from animism by selling goats and cows for sacrifices. When some of the women became Christians, their husbands beat them, but they did not give up their new faith.

About 1980, an American missionary named Mark Nichol moved to our area to spread the gospel, and he stayed with our tribe for about fifteen years, living in a grass hut just like we did and learning to speak Dinka perfectly. He gave us supplies and shared the gospel by preaching to large groups and one-on-one with anyone who would listen. The adults ignored him at first, but we children listened because he gave us candy. We did not understand all that he said at first; we were especially confused when he held a cross and showed pictures of a white man named Jesus. At that time, I did not understand who Jesus was—I thought he was showing us pictures of his relative, but I did not know why. As his following grew, he began holding regular Sunday services and Sunday school so that he could equip others to help him spread the gospel to our tribesmen. He wanted to build a school, but the war stopped him.

As time passed, increasing numbers of young men and women began to worship Jesus Christ, and during the early 1980s, the older men finally began to adopt the new belief system too. Unfortunately, I believe some people only became

Christians because sacrificing to the traditional gods was expensive. Christianity was easy—it cost nothing to please God because salvation was a free gift. After the war started, some people became Christians simply to spite the Muslims, who absolutely hated Christianity. Nevertheless, church choirs were formed, and people traveled day and night from house to house and village to village to burn the huts and implements that had been used for magic. Most people stopped sacrificing to gods, and bulls were killed for food or for marriage ceremonies because they were no longer held sacred. After 1982, my clan stopped visiting its god, Deng-Pajerbe, and the sacrificial bulls for the next year were butchered on Christmas Day in the church so that the meat could be shared with the other villagers. By the close of the 1980s, almost everyone in southern Sudan called themselves Christians.

However, because the new converts could not read the Bible, they had no way of learning about Christian living except by listening to the missionaries; therefore, they mixed their new beliefs with some of their animistic traditions, especially when bad weather or disease threatened them. I remember one terrible drought when half the village prayed and the other half sacrificed animals because they thought a collective effort by both religions would bring rain. Many people did not even know how to pray, so they often said confused prayers like, "Are you really the god who can help us?"

When the Muslims in the north heard that Christianity was rapidly spreading in the south, they began to visit our villages, bringing many beautiful gifts to win our loyalty. Local chiefs were their first targets, so the Muslims brought them Islamic clothes, salt, sugar, umbrellas, and other items to convince them how generous and good their religion was. Once, two trucks full of gifts were brought to our village and passed out among us. I was given a white gown, the Islamic dress for men. Muslims began shouting "Allah Akbar" very loudly, but no one responded back to them. They told us we needed to say "Allah Akbar" before they would give us something, so we did what we were told to get the gifts, but we did not convert to Islam. I was surprised when I heard my father tell my mother, "These Muslims are stupid! Do they think we will become Muslims for these items they have brought us?" I was too young to understand why my father criticized good people who gave us such nice things for free.

One other time, when Islamic preachers were expected in our village, many people gathered together first and conspired to say "Alleluia" if the Muslims said "Allah Akbar." When the preachers arrived and began their rally, they became very angry at our responses. They tried for a short time to convince us to change our minds, but they finally gave up, boarded their plane, and flew back to the north. I think that made them very hostile to our region so that, later, when the war broke out, government troops were especially cruel to us because they called our villages "areas of devils."

As I grew, I realized that all the families had to pay taxes to the government, but no one knew what the government did with the money because they did not build any schools, roads, or hospitals in our community. Every year I heard my father complain that he had to sell a cow to pay our taxes. He began to include me in his discussions with my mother to choose which cow should be sold, although I did not have much to say when I was so young. One year we were even taxed twice because the government told us their officials had lost our payments; we had no choice but to pay them again. That was the first hint I had that the government was treating us unfairly.

Then began what I now call "the bloody digging of the Jonglei Canal."

In the 1980s, the Sudanese government joined hands with Egypt to dig a canal to improve drainage of the Nile River valley and to increase the flow of the Nile. They decided that agriculture in both Sudan and Egypt would benefit by the Jonglei Canal, but the leaders neglected to involve the people in the south when the project was planned. When southerners living in the north found out that their homeland was going to be affected, they began to protest by holding marches. To silence them, the government broke up the marches, arresting and jailing some of the protestors, killing and throwing others in the river for the fish and crocodiles to feed on. When one fisherman in the south found a body floating in the river, we began to realize how dangerous the government was. More demonstrators were arrested, but no one could find where they were jailed. Three months later, the Government of Sudan announced that they released all the protestors, but relatives waited in vain—their loved ones never returned home.

Soon the work began in southern Sudan. The CCI engineering company from France was hired to dig the canal. Using their powerful machine called a "bucket wheel," they carved a trench about sixty feet deep and a third of a mile wide. Beginning in Malakal, they covered over one mile per week on their way to the Nile River at Bor Town.

I was six years old when the bucket wheel arrived in our village. Fascinated, I watched the huge machine throw the mud far from the trench, the noise from the engine traveling for miles over the quiet African plains. My father complained about the destructive project, hating the damage done to the land, but I secretly enjoyed the activity—until the bulldozer reached our home. Two days later, our home, our farm, and our fields were destroyed, only one month before harvest. The bulldozers made us all homeless, without protection from the mosquitoes and the coming rainy season. The effects were far reaching, especially the harm to our food supply. Our desert climate has only one growing season, so we lost our only chance for a crop that year. We also lost our grass barns called "luak" that protected up to thirty-five cows each from the lions, hyenas, tigers, and other wild animals.

We waited, expecting payment for our losses, but no one came to compensate us. We were not able to communicate with the workers who destroyed our homes because we did not speak Arabic or French. Eventually, we found one worker from the south who could translate our questions to the French fore-man. The white man told us to ask our government for pay-ment because the company had already paid them for the dam-ages. We could not pursue the matter because we were afraid the government would silence us with their guns, just as they had silenced the protestors. Our elders remembered the bloody rebellion in 1956. Our tribes had used spears and arrows to fight government troops armed with guns. Many chiefs, inno-cent villagers, and rebels were killed, including one of the lead-ers, Deng Nhial. As the soldiers were searching for rebels, they looted cattle and raped women. My father told me about the time his cousin was caught and hanged because the soldiers found many spears in his hut and thought he was a rebel. Out of fear, we remained silent.

In addition to the loss of our property, the canal work-ers were responsible for the loss of human lives because they were very careless with their equipment. Once I watched in horror as a drunken Muslim driver crushed a mother and her four children. Right after the accident, I saw the driver smil-ing to his friends, seemingly happy with his "mistake." One of the victims survived for a while, but she died after a few days because no one took her to a hospital. The black Christians in the south were not believed to be important, so the company did not take any responsibility for the accident. The only compensation given to the mourners consisted of packages of salt and cooking oil. Some villagers said the family was "lucky" because other families did not receive anything for the loss of their loved ones.

That year many villagers became sick and died from mosquito bites, and starvation followed since our crops were destroyed. The bucket wheel dug on, but it never finished the canal because the war broke out when it had only completed about 260 kilometers out of the total distance of 360 kilometers. The bucket wheel was abandoned until it was burned by angry villagers in 1986.

While we were too afraid to fight against the corrupt government, others in the north were not. Trouble was brewing because the Muslims who controlled the government were making it increasingly difficult for non-Muslims to get an education or employment. My cousin who attended high school in Malakal told me that people were forced to convert to Islam before they could attend college or get a job, so a few southern Sudanese who worked for the government and university students from the south made plans to overthrow the Islamic government.

The war started on May 16, 1983, when a band of Christian southerners led by John Garang rebelled against government forces in the town of Bor in the upper Nile region. A lot of victims, especially Arab traders and officials, were captured and killed during the uprising. In retaliation, the government sent more troops from the north to Bor to kill the rebels. When the soldiers found that those who had launched the attack were gone, they killed civilians instead, throwing their bodies into the Nile.

Since Bor is about two hundred miles from my village, we did not hear about the fight until three days later. Shortly after that, I saw government warplanes flying overhead for the first time; I thought they were big birds until my father told me they were machines piloted by men. The noise of their engines frightened me, but I kept watching because I was so amazed. The planes flew above us for several hours until they turned northward without harming us.

Later that week, I was tending the cattle and playing with the other boys in a field a few miles outside our village when we heard the planes returning. This time, they were armed. We heard the explosions in the distance, and we saw the dark smoke rise from village after village. We had no idea what was happening until the planes found our herds and began dropping their bombs on our cattle, killing most of them and scattering the rest. My friends and I survived only because we were playing away from the herds where we were not noticed. At first, we ran toward the cattle to control them because we thought they were just afraid of the engine noise, but we soon realized what was happening when we saw the ground sprayed with blood and the chunks of meat that landed near us. We gaped at the animals as they lay dying, blowing blood out of their mouths and nostrils. Terrified, we ran home to tell our parents without stopping to look for the few cows that had scattered. Finally, the planes turned north, and the sky was quiet again.

When I reached my home, I asked my mother where my father was. Tearfully, she explained that he had gone to help our neighbors and friends who had been injured or killed in the attack. I did not know what to do. I was afraid to go to him because I did not want to see blood again, but I was eager to tell him about our cattle. I decided to wait for him to come home, so I went to sleep. He was home when I woke, but he was not as upset as I thought he would be when I told him that more than ten of our cows were gone. He was more angry and saddened that he had seen people die.

The government succeeded in their main objective: to destroy many of the cattle we needed as our main source of food. After that, we tried to hide our remaining cattle in the thick forests, but they were hard to control there. We boys were afraid to follow our herds because we often saw planes flying a few feet from the ground as the pilots looked for cattle, people, huts, and stores to destroy. Without herders, the cattle wandered wherever they wanted, often falling prey to wild animals. The year 1985 was named "The Year of Starvation" because most of our crops and cattle were destroyed by the Government of Sudan. We had nothing to eat except wild vegetables and fruits. The small children and elderly quickly became malnourished and died because they did not have the strength to survive.

Once, as my father went to hunt for food, he was ambushed, robbed, beaten, and left for dead by the government militia. Even the birds thought he was dead and came to feed on him, but he was able to move slightly to scare them away. No one among my father's wives knew where he was, so he lay in the dust for many hours. Finally, some people hiding in the nearby bushes saw flocks of vultures gathering near him, waiting for him to die. Hoping to find a dead animal they could feed to their families, they came running and found my father in a pool of blood. They recognized him and brought him to our hiding place. We had hoped to see him return with food for us, so we were shocked to see him covered with his own blood— his mouth, eyes, and nose sealed shut. My mother cleaned him in warm water, but his wounds were too deep in his head, face, back, and chest. We had no medicine, so we used cow urine to kill the germs. I sat next to him for days, shooing the flies from his wounds. He could not speak or move except to cough and sneeze the blood from his nose. Christians came every morning and evening to pray quietly for his life, being careful not to be heard by the enemy. Thankfully, their prayers were answered; in only a few months, his wounds were healed, and he was able to speak and walk again. Everyone said he was a lucky person to survive such a brutal attack. Many other men beaten like he was never recovered.

My father decided he could no longer hide with us because the militia would kill us all—women and children—if they found him with us, so he left us to find his own hiding place. The government had learned that John Garang, the leader of rebels in the south, had grown up in a village about fifty miles from our village and that many of the young men in our region were joining the rebellion. When the soldiers came to ask where to find Garang's parents and other relatives, they began killing everyone who would not cooperate with them. Garang fueled the killing by sending armed rebels to fight the government troops, but the rebels were defeated and no living being was spared—even chickens and dogs were slaughtered. The government soldiers also planted land mines in every path before they moved on.

This was the first time I had seen so many human inventions, and I was amazed at the technology of weapons of destruction—guns, bombs, airplanes, and land mines. To survive, we had to move to the banks of the Nile to live in the tall grass and to fish in the thick reeds where the ground was too swampy for the government vehicles to navigate. We felt safer, but many died from disease from the mosquitoes in the swamps, and others starved because they did not have fishing nets or hooks to catch enough fish. People stayed awake during the night to swat the mosquitoes and slept during the day when it was too hot for the pests to bite. Some of our own rebels looted food, clothing, and mosquito netting from the local people. When the Nile flooded, the government troops moved to the cities, so my mother brought us back home to find our huts had been burned. We were glad that she was able to build a new hut to protect us from wild animals and mosquitoes.

My father had been gone for almost a year, so we thought he must be dead. We lived in fear because a few militia groups still roamed the area, stealing and killing. Sometimes they burned people alive as they slept in their huts at night, so we were terrified one night when a voice outside our window woke us. Fearing for our lives, my mother did not respond. The voice called my mother's name several times before she recognized it was my father whispering very slowly to her. The night was dark, so he could sit outside the window without being seen. He would not enter the hut because he feared being caught. He talked for quite a while, encouraging my mother to take good care of us. She began to cry, and then we all cried, not knowing if we would ever see him again. Finally, he slipped away from the hut into the night, and I would not see him for several years.

The whole region was in chaos—my peaceful village in southern Sudan was changed forever. The government militias roamed the south, capturing and imprisoning innocent farmers and ranchers without trials; some of my neighbors went to join the rebels who were fighting for their homeland, but many more went into hiding in the bushes to suffer from hunger and illness while they waited for their wives and children to bring them food and water when the soldiers were not watching. Families lived apart, hoping some of them could survive. Life as we had known it ceased. There were no wrestling matches, traditional dances, or even marriages. Searching for food, mourning the dead, and digging graves were our only activities in the south. Unknown to them, the government militias actually helped us avoid starvation because they killed elephants for their ivory tusks, but they left the carcasses in the dust for us to find and eat. We heard that people from the Barghazel region fled from the Jangjweed Arab militiamen by moving to the upper Nile region. They thought they would be safe there, but they found it was a worse war zone than the one they had left.

For years the abuses continued. One day in 1986, a group of Arabs armed with AK-47 rifles and kitchen knives came to the house of my twelve-year-old friend, Jamal, who lived with his parents, another woman, and his siblings. The men were dressed in fatigues of the People's Defence Forces (PDF), which identified them as soldiers of the Jihad who had been fighting in the south. The soldiers told Jamal, his brother, and his father that they were wanted at the police station for questioning because someone in the neighborhood had reported a theft. Confident in their innocence, the three men agreed to go with the soldiers to the police station, so they willingly climbed into the soldiers' pick-up truck.

Thirty minutes later, the truck stopped in the open desert. The soldiers dragged Jamal, his father, and his brother from the truck and tied ropes around their necks. The other ends of the ropes were tied to the truck, and the soldiers drove around the desert, dragging the bodies behind them. The sadistic soldiers enjoyed the agony and the helplessness of their victims until their bodies went limp and their screaming stopped. The soldiers untied the ropes and left the three bodies lying in the desert sun and returned to town for more victims. Jamal's father and brother were dead, but Jamal was still barely breathing.

At midnight, the soldiers went to the house of Deng, who was fifty years old. When he came to the door, one soldier told him he was wanted by Jamal's family to bail them out of jail. Deng was a friend of Jamal's family, so he did not hesitate to go with the soldiers. Again, as soon as Deng took his seat, the Toyota truck immediately sped off toward the desert. First, the soldiers tortured him; then he, too, was tied to the bumper of the truck and dragged around the hard desert ground. They tossed his limp body with its shredded skin and bloody buttocks, thighs, abdomen, and arms next to Jamal's body.

Hours later, the cool breeze of the early morning woke Deng. He opened his eyes but could not move his body that burned with pain. He tried to call out, but his voice was weak. As he tried again, Jamal slowly opened his eyes and responded. They recognized each other immediately, but they were barely able to communicate because their throats were swollen from the ropes. Jamal was unable to move, but Deng became determined to use the last energy he had to limp all the way back to town. Fortunately, when he reached the road, a car stopped, and the driver took him to the police. As Deng was choking out his story to the police chief, another police officer walked into the room. Deng immediately recognized him as one of soldiers who had abducted and tortured him. Both the chief of police and the officer denied that the police had been involved. Deng was told to arrange a party to celebrate his survival instead of accusing others.

Still in terrible pain, Deng led the police back to the desert where they found Jamal still alive, so the two survivors were taken to a clinic by the policemen. Further searching in the area revealed many human bones and skulls that had been left there for the birds. Those responsible for the crimes were never arrested; the authorities simply turn a blind eye to the crimes.

I witnessed other bloody acts of violence. Once masked men went from door to door, arresting twenty black male southerners. Their families and relatives reported to the government authorities that armed soldiers in Jihad uniforms had ordered them out of their houses at gunpoint, but the authorities denied the kidnapping charges and said that the men might have simply decided to run away to join the rebellion. Days later, the twenty headless bodies were found miles away from town; the heads of the victims were never found.

Disappearances like those were happening in many areas of the Sudan. People were shot on the streets, but no one was arrested for their murders. Some were jailed and were never seen again. Thousands simply disappeared. Hand grenades or rockets were thrown into houses at night to silence the families who were complaining to government officials. The best way to find a missing relative was to wake up every morning and look toward the desert sky to see if birds were flying over a corpse. Then, at least, the relatives could find the bones of their loved ones.

In the mid-1980s, the government began organizing militia groups by releasing convicted prisoners from jails and gathering homeless thieves from the cities in the north. These convicts and thieves were given Islamic uniforms used for fighting holy wars, and they were sent into the south and paid to kill Christians for the Islamic government. They were told that they would be well paid for their genocide and that they could confiscate all the possessions they wanted from people they killed.

In addition, government helicopters delivered beer and marijuana to the militia, so they committed terrible acts when they were drunk or high on drugs. They developed methods of torture in which they needled the testes of male prisoners to force them to reveal the hiding places of other southern Sudanese. The pain was so intense that prisoners would sometimes make up information to tell the soldiers. Some victims of such torturing became impotent and others died. The soldiers were able to capture many others by using the information gathered in these brutal interrogations. Those who went into hiding could not tell their hiding places to their relatives and neighbors for fear of being betrayed to the enemy.

One of the most tragic examples of brutality happened in 1984 in a village close to mine where a mother and her five children were hiding in the bushes. Two of her children were too young to understand that they were in danger and that they should be quiet, so the mother tried in vain to keep them still. As the soldiers passed by their hiding place, the two-year-old girl smiled brightly, waved her little hand, and cheerfully said, "Hello!" to the men. She added, "Could you carry me back home to play? My mother makes me walk because she usually carries my younger brother when we come to hide and when we return home at night." Her family tried to silence her, but it was too late. The little girl happily pointed her finger and asked her mother to stand up so they could go home. Without hesitating, the soldiers opened fire on the family, killing them all—including the young girls. Other villagers hiding nearby saw what happened and spread the word that not even the lives of innocent babies were spared.

Over time, more and more soldiers and militiamen arrived in the villages in the upper Nile region and made life even more difficult for the tribes than it had been before. The villagers typically obtained their water from swamps during the rainy season and from a "borehole" that served as a community well during the summer. The few water holes were often many miles apart, which made it difficult to get water to drink and to give to livestock. Sometimes families spent the entire day standing in long lines for their turn to draw water from the well hole.

Because water was so scarce, the government tried to control the people by controlling the water supply. In 1985, when rebels started attacking government troops, soldiers were positioned at the boreholes that served many villages. The women had no other alternative than to come to the well to get their water, but they were often raped or captured by the soldiers. Mothers were powerless to protect themselves and their children from the soldiers, who enjoyed torturing the young boys to force them to reveal their fathers' whereabouts and to identify which family members had joined the rebels. The boys often made false accusations so that the soldiers would stop the torture, so many people were arrested and slaughtered in front of crowds without investigations or trials. In some areas, many people and cattle died from dehydration because the government troops did not allow them to draw any water from the community wells.

One year, in the area of Patheng, a great travesty occurred when government troops heard about a successful rebel attack that had killed many Muslim soldiers. As revenge, all the women and children of the village were told to sit down in rows to make drawing the water easier, but the armed troops stood in front of them and opened fire on the innocent villagers. Only a few escaped. To make matters worse, the soldiers threw all the dead bodies into the borehole to intentionally ruin the only water source of the area. Those troops moved and joined camps at other boreholes, but the remaining villagers were left without a clean-water source. The following morning, when the survivors returned to identify their loved ones' bodies, all they found were vultures trying to get the dead flesh out of the well. The bodies could not be removed from the well, so they were left there, unidentified.

The message was immediately spread that no one should drink from the contaminated borehole, so the thirsty villagers decided that they must walk almost one hundred miles to another borehole. They abandoned their homes, leaving all their possessions behind except for containers to carry water. The healthy girls and boys who could run were sent ahead to get water for the younger children and the elderly who had to walk very slowly. Luckily, when word spread that they were coming, nearby villagers carried water for the thirsty travelers. Some who stayed behind died before water could be brought back to them, but some were rescued.

As time went on, the abuses escalated. Armed soldiers burned houses and churches to the ground, and they killed and raped many innocent women and children—some as many as five times a day. The Arabs called the young black Christians the "children of devils," and they told the women that raping them would improve the quality of the next generation because the skin of their children would be lighter from their Arab fathers. They said that Sudan is an Arab nation that suffers shame because of the black Christians in the south.

Some of the soldiers kept women as slaves for themselves in their camps, and other women, men, and children were taken to the north to be sold in Arab slave markets. As a result, the militia groups increased their kidnappings because they could make easy money in the slave trade. At this time, the demand for boys and girls in the slave market increased because boys were wanted to perform hard physical labor, and girls were desired as sex slaves. Most of these young victims could not escape because they were locked up and did not know how to find their way home, but a few did manage to escape and return safely to the south. Their stories shocked their families. They told how their masters had beaten and starved them and how many of their friends died in their slavery.

More villages were attacked, so the people lived in fear of the government and tried to hide from the soldiers to escape being raped and sold into slavery. The torture of young boys for information increased, and starvation spread because people could not openly farm or raise their animals for food. The government troops and militia took all the cattle, the primary food source, to the north as their property. Local food stores were burned to ashes, as well as homes. People captured and accused of rebellion were used for militia training when they were tied to trees and used for target practice. The government ordered that all churches and all Christian symbols must be burned. Sunday Christian services were outlawed, and the militias shot worshippers who were caught gathering for prayer.

Besides the violence, the Muslims tried to convince the people in the south to renounce their Christian beliefs and convert to Islam. The soldiers preached to the people that Mohammed, not Jesus, is the true Son of God who was born by the Holy Spirit. They told us that Mary had made up the story of the Immaculate Conception because she was a prostitute from the west who had slept with so many men that she did not know who had conceived her child, Jesus. They also showed pictures of Jesus to the southerners to convince them that Jesus could not have been God's son because he was white. They argued that the southerners were black, so Mohammed must be the Son of God because he was dark skinned too.

Despite the risk, we southerners refused to proclaim that Mohammed was God's son, and we refused to pray five times a day to Allah. We Christians saw Islam as a religion of racism because it forbids the translation of the Koran into any language besides Arabic. In contrast, we saw Christianity as a system of belief that embraced all cultures. Our rejection of Islam angered the Muslims, so the abuses intensified.

About this time, my father appeared and told my stepmother that she should take me to hide with her along the Nile River. Many boys my age were living in the swampy areas with their families, too, because the government troops could not drive their vehicles into the soggy area and the reeds would protect us from being seen by the warplanes. My mother could not come with me because my younger siblings were not able to stand the mosquitoes and other insects by the river, so they had to stay back on the dry land. My father hid so far away from us that he could only visit us about once a month. I did not asked where he was hiding because I did not want to know. I feared that the government troops might find me and torture me, so I did not want to be able to betray him as other boys had betrayed their fathers.

JOURNEY 2: FROM SUDAN TO ETHIOPIA

By 1987, the entire region of southern Sudan was in turmoil because the government troops had destroyed our social stability. Only a few children had parents because most of the adults had been killed or sold into slavery. Homeless children roamed the country, fighting for survival and hiding from the soldiers who tortured and killed them because the government feared that the young boys would join the rebellion when they grew up. Hiding was difficult for many boys because they feared the wild animals in the bushes.

In early summer, several boys who had been hiding for two years came up with the idea that they should walk out of the country because they were tired of living in fear of the government. As they made their plans, other boys decided to join them because they believed they would be safer in Ethiopia, just as other refugees had been during Sudan's first Civil War in 1956.

Once the decision was made, the message spread rapidly to each tribe that all the boys would walk together to Ethiopia. Many of the boys were orphans, but some still had parents who feared that their sons would suffer on the journey and would not be welcome in their new country. Some parents could not bear the thought of losing their children, so they did not tell their boys about the trip. When their boys found out, the parents denied knowing about the plan. By July 1987, the word had spread throughout the south.

At that time, I was still hiding by the Nile where the government vehicles could not come, but I was tired of living in the soggy grass with vicious insects. Even though we were fairly hidden from the soldiers, we were not safe because wild animals such as crocodiles and hippopotami attacked us at night, so when some men came to fish for food and told us that many boys had decided to walk out of the country, I was eager to join the group. Before I could decide, though, I wanted to ask my family. A few days later when my father visited us, I told him I needed to leave with the other boys, but he did not answer me at first. The next day, he admitted that I might be better off in Ethiopia because he could not protect me from the soldiers—he could barely protect himself—and he admitted that he could not stop me from leaving with the other boys. When evening covered us, he took me to my mother's hiding place. My family was very glad to see me again, until my father told them I had to join the boys leaving the country. They were shocked—especially because the boys were planning to leave in about a week. My mother was so upset that she refused to see me off on the day of the journey. We left her in hiding, and my father took me to meet the other boys from my village.

The decision to leave was very difficult, but we had no choice because we had nothing left to support ourselves; everything we needed to survive was gone—our cattle and water had been taken, and we could not raise food to eat. If we remained in the country, we knew we would be killed or sold into slavery. Many had seen their parents and other loved ones slaughtered in front of them, so they had no hope left. Thousands of boys, twelve years old and younger, agreed to begin our journey as soon as possible because Sudan was no longer safe for us.

Preparing for the trip was not easy because we needed many supplies for the harsh journey through the desert of Ajageer with its rocky, hard ground. Important items such as food, mosquito netting, shoes, and clothing had been looted by the government troops, and there were no markets or money to purchase what we needed. Some of us were able to scrounge some supplies, but no one was fully prepared. My father gave me some food, a mosquito net, and a small plastic sheet to protect myself from the rain. Compared to many of the other boys who had no families to help them, I was well prepared. Nevertheless, we would all have to trust God to protect us from starvation and danger.

As preparations were being made, the elders held meetings in each community to encourage us boys that we were not outcasts from their people, but that we were being sent away for our own protection. We were told to think of ourselves as seeds that would be planted in new ground if God helped us cross to Ethiopia. The day for the journey to Ethiopia was decided, and messengers ran throughout the south for days, telling all the boys when and where to meet for the journey.

When the day arrived, all the villagers met to pray and to sing songs of sorrow. Mothers and sons clung to each other, crying tears of good-bye. Some women went into shock; some men were so weak with grief that they could not stand. The crying and wailing was loud as they watched what they never could have imagined: thousand of children traveling by themselves to a strange land. Words cannot express the pain of that day. My father hugged me many times as he said good-bye. One of the elders killed a bull as a sign of blessing, and each of us leapt over it and walked away, our families watching and wailing until the dust hid us from view. We had become the Lost Boys of Sudan.

As we walked through the desert, the air was quiet and dry. The sun beat mercilessly as we trudged over the hot ground dotted with only a few small trees. Each boy carried heavy containers of drinking water because we knew that no rain would fall during the dry season. The stronger boys helped to carry the possessions of those who were very young, sick, or weak, so that the group could walk quickly. The path was rocky and rough; those without shoes felt their bare feet swell and ache. Soon, their feet began to bleed, but they had no choice but to limp painfully on.

In less than three days, many boys ran out of food, so they ate whatever they could find along the way. As a result, some died from eating wild fruit and leaves that filled their stomachs but poisoned their systems. Others collapsed or broke their legs when they fell into holes. No one had medicine to help them, so we had to leave them behind. We grieved over our decision, but we were too young and weak to carry the sick and crippled across the hot desert. We needed to walk quickly because wild animals such as hyenas, lions, and other carnivores attacked those who lagged behind. Without weapons, we could not prevent the hungry lions from killing the boys who could not run away. We also feared that soldiers might appear at any moment, so we moved as quickly as we could to cover the long distances between water holes, avoiding the areas that might have soldiers.

As our water ran out, many of the boys died from dehydration in the hot desert. The rest of us trudged on in groups of two or three while some walked alone because fatigue and thirst weakened them. We survived by drinking our own urine until we finally saw trees in the distance, two-and-a-half weeks after leaving home. We rejoiced to see green leaves and branches filled with different types of birds. The swamp water underneath the trees was filthy with animal waste, but we did not care—it was the water we needed to survive.

Those who arrived first drank in the dirty water, quickly filled their containers, and ran back to rescue the other boys left behind in the desert. Some were reached in time, but others had died or wandered away. A few had decided to turn around and go back home. No one knows how many boys died because no one kept records. After a few hours at the swamp, we found lion tracks, so we decided we could stay no longer. We knew the animals would return and attack, so we took final drinks, filled our containers with the dirty water, and continued on.

As we walked through Sudan, some of the tribes began calling us "lost kids" in their dialects. Most of the natives were friendly, but, at one point, we had to pass through the area of the Murle tribe, a harsh group who had formed a militia armed by the Government of Sudan to fight against the uprising in the south. Their main trade was stealing children from other tribes and selling them to families who needed children. The one aspect of the Murle culture that helped to protect us was that Murles do not walk outside their villages at night unless they are forced to because they believed that anyone killed while walking at night had no excuse to blame the killer.

Therefore, we waited during the day in the bushes miles away from Murle territory. Worried and fearful, we gathered at about six o'clock p.m. When night fell, we began walking fifty miles across the land of our enemies. When the sun rose ten hours later, we were almost to the border of Murle territory when we were attacked by members of the tribe.

Some of us escaped and scattered in groups of two and three. Luckily, a few met some of the rebel soldiers from the town of Pibor. When we told them what was happening, the soldiers immediately took their guns and ran to save the rest. The battle was fierce, but the rebels succeeded in driving off the Murles. Many boys had been killed; many had been kidnapped, and some had been injured and left to die; nevertheless, we felt God had miraculously saved the rest of us by sending the rebels to fight for us.

After the fight, the rebel soldiers began looking for the boys who had run away, but the boys hid from the men, thinking they were government militia. Some of us traveled with the rebel soldiers so that the other boys would see them and come out of hiding. At the same time, the government militias were also searching for the boys, so occasional gunfire broke out between the two factions.

Two days later, many dead bodies were found in the bushes, victims of dehydration and starvation because we had lost our food and water during the Murle attack. Our blankets, mosquito nets, food, and cooking utensils had been taken by the enemy. The clothes we were wearing were the only property we had left, and there were no supplies to be had in Pibor because the rebels themselves were just barely surviving by eating wild fruits, vegetables, and leaves. A number of boys suffered mentally and emotionally because of the attacks and the memories of their murdered friends. Others had nightmares that woke them, and they ran into bushes at night, thinking they were being attacked again. The rest of us were designated to guard the sick and stand watch during the night. A number of boys died from infections because there were no medicine or bandages to treat their bullet wounds. After a few days, the rebels decided that they should all return to town because the wild plants for food were getting scarce and no more Lost Boys were being found.

We only spent four days in Pibor before resuming our journey because there was a rumor that the government militia was planning another attack to capture more boys for trade. Before we left, the local people frequently came to town, hoping to exchange five kilos of meat for a boy. They knew we were starving, so the natives hoped we would be willing to sell some of our group into slavery. We were horrified and sent the people away, but some of us began to worry that the bigger, stronger boys might become desperate enough to actually agree to sell some of the smaller boys. We also worried that the local people might try to kidnap some of us since they could not buy boys. On the fourth night in Pibor, we quietly prepared to leave to avoid detection by the enemy. Those who were sick or injured would remain with the rebels in Pibor Town because they would not be able to walk. We never found out what happened to those friends we left behind.

Fearing another attack from the Murles, we walked quietly in the dark, being very careful not to cough, talk, or sneeze. The Pibor rebel authorities assigned ten soldiers to escort us safely out of the territory, five men leading the way, five men protecting the rear of the group. They organized themselves in family groups of five to ten boys headed by the oldest boys, who were twelve years old. Most of the leaders took their roles very seriously, denying themselves food so the weak and sick could have more. We served each other in peace and unity to please God.

When we stopped to rest, five of the soldiers stood guard while the other five hunted wild game, and we boys gathered whatever wild fruit we could find. Luckily, many gazelles grazed in the area, so the rebels were able to feed the twelve thousand boys by roasting the meat on open fires. There was plenty of water to drink, but it was very dirty and full of insects and frog eggs. Our group walked for twenty days before reaching the Anyuak tribe close to the Ethiopian border.

It was a chilly morning when we reached the Ajuara River that separated us from Anyuak villages. Walking through the thick bushes and long grass of the riverbank, we found a swift-flowing river that was too deep for us to walk across. A few of the strongest swimmers made it safely to the other side, but some were washed downstream because they were too weak to fight the current. Most of us did not know how to swim, so the ten adults began carrying boys across. They finished eighteen hours later, said good-bye to the boys, and headed back to Pibor because they were needed to fight in the resistance movement. Once again, we Lost Boys were on our own.

We continued on toward the land of the Anyuak tribe. Fearful, we worried that the Anyuak people might want to capture us to use for bait because they trapped tigers to use the valuable fur for dowries. Hunting with spears was too difficult, so the natives injected poison into dead bodies to bait the tigers and kill them. Thankfully, our fears were unfounded because the villagers did not know we were coming. When the Anyuak saw so many of us children coming to their land without adults, they became frightened themselves. The natives ran from us—naked, bloody boys who were as thin as skeletons and looked like wild animals ready to eat anything in our path. As the message spread, every village was evacuated, so we were able to walk safely through the area. While a few of the natives stood at a distance to watch, some of the boys in our group tried shouting to them, asking directions to Ethiopia. Unfortunately, the Anyuaks could not understand our language and thought the boys were asking the way to "Thuya" instead of Ethiopia. When some of us asked for food, the selfish Anyuaks threw food to their dogs instead of to us.

Eventually, a few among the Anyuak tribe figured out that that we were not dangerous animals but just scared, hungry refugees looking for safety. The Anyuaks communicated that they were willing to trade food for the clothes we were wearing.

We were so hungry that one boy in each group of five agreed to exchange his t-shirt and shorts for the stale food that he shared with the other four boys in his group. Each day, another boy traded his clothes until every Lost Boy was naked. Some boys were left behind because they were so weak from starvation that they could not walk.

When we ran out of clothing to trade, finding food became harder and harder. We did not know how far we had left to travel, and we longed for their journey to end. We had hoped to find food in the town of Pochalla, but we only found more hungry people from southern Sudan. The good news was that there were no government militia or troops there, so we were safe, even though we were still hungry.

After one night in Pochalla, three of the southern Sudanese led us toward Ethiopia. For ten days, we traveled slowly, eating only raw leaves and fruits. Our mouths turned dark green; speaking became so difficult that some could only communicate with their tears. As we reached the southwest border between Sudan and Ethiopia, we were relieved to find only a deep river—no roadblocks or police would stop us. Looking across the divide, we saw a building with a metal roof shining in the bright, clear day. We rejoiced that our safe haven was so close—our hopes were almost fulfilled! The only obstacle remaining was the Funyido River. A few boys managed to swim the distance, but most of us were too weak to attempt it. We simply lay down on the beach, tired and helpless.

When the Ethiopian villagers saw the boys who reached their shore, they came running to help with two boats, each able to carry fifteen boys at a time. Unfortunately, one of the boatmen was cruel. When his full boat was in the middle of the river, he purposely capsized it. He laughed as the weak children drowned in the deep water. No one tried to help them—the man only brought his boat to shore.

After that, the rest of the boys refused to climb into the boats until an elderly man and woman came across the river to them. The couple could not communicate with words, but they motioned for about thirty minutes, pointing to their gray hair and the sky. Finally, we realized that the couple was telling us to trust them because they were old and they feared God. The couple put better people in charge of the boats and convinced the boys to get into the boats. The ferrying began again at about eight o'clock a.m. and continued throughout the day and into the night. Finally, at midnight, the last of the Lost Boys left the Sudan and started their new lives in a new land.

Our hope for a better life soon began to fade as we were faced with the harsh reality of our new home. The bright building that had appeared in the distance turned out to be the only one in the town of Funyido, and it offered no hope for us. The building was divided in two; one side was used for Sunday worship by only a few people in an area with more than ten thousand. The other side was used as a bar where the locals drank and gambled. Unfortunately, the Ethiopians did not want to be responsible for the scores of starving children struggling between life and death. Many villagers gathered to watch and make fun of us, the naked skeletons with physical deformities and gaping wounds.

The villagers forced us boys into the bushes and trees about ten miles from their village. Without tools to clear the bushes, we lived like animals in the wild. The mosquitoes, spiders, scorpions, and other insects constantly tormented us, and the snakes and animals made our lives miserable. Many of the boys lost their hope and courage as our situation worsened. Finding food and gathering wild plants was not easy because the dry season had turned the leaves of every plant to yellow, except for a few trees that could not be eaten. Diseases such as cholera claimed the lives of many. Digging graves was difficult without tools, so we simply piled the dead bodies at a distance. Flies carried more disease from the dead to the living, and the smell from the rotting bodies became familiar to us young refugees. The few trees provided our only shelter for sleeping at night and avoiding the hot sun during the day.

We did our best to make life bearable by collecting rusted cans to use for cooking plant leaves and carrying water from the river. Some could not open their mouths because they had not eaten for a long time, but they forced themselves to eat the sour leaves of the plants. As a result, their mouths became infected, and their stomachs convulsed with pain. Without hospitals or clinics to relieve their suffering, they struggled to survive without help.

As more and more boys starved to death, the survivors continued to pile the dead bodies, and the vultures and jackals came to feed on the carcasses. The flocks perched in the trees during the night as we slept underneath. The bird droppings fell on us, in our food, and in our water. After the first few days, the smell of rotten bodies and animal waste kept the local children from coming to abuse and mock us suffering Sudanese children, but some still waited at the river to laugh at the naked skeletons who came to quench their thirst and cool off under the shade of the trees along the river. The locals taunted us by calling us "Ajuil," which means "small animals without homes." The Anyuak youth entertained themselves with the cruel pleasure of pushing the sick boys into the river, watching them cry for help as they drowned. The locals showed no pity and made no effort to rescue the weak ones from the water. We quickly learned to fear the river and to stay back where the stench of the bodies kept the others away.

Flashbacks were bitter and painful. South Sudan was no longer our home, and we grieved the loss of our loved ones and the kind people we had met on our journey. Waiting to die became our single pastime. The destination that had given us the strength to trudge miles and miles through desert and jungle to escape the evils of government troops and militia was not a safe haven—it was simply another place of suffering. When we slept, we relived the horrible scenes of our loved ones being slaughtered in the streets, and when we awoke, we lived in the terror and pain of starvation, disease, and cruelty.

Some of the boys tried to bring hope to the others by turning to God. All of us were Christians, but we were young and did not know how to lead Sunday worship services. We sang sad songs in our various dialects, and we cried out to God to deliver us from our hardships and to heal our wounds and diseases. Some attempted to attend the local church one Sunday, but the people sent them away because they smelled of death and filth. A few were literally thrown out of the church and returned to our camp with new injuries from hitting the hard ground.

Some boys began to work for food by collecting firewood for the local people, but cheating the helpless boys happened more often than not. The boys could gather wood as many as ten times a day to please their master and to receive one meal, but the majority were forced away by their masters after delivering the wood and receiving nothing in return. The boys gambled when they trusted the locals because they never knew if they would be paid or not.

After a month, a truck filled with maize came to rescue us, but the deliverymen were repulsed by the horrible smell of the dead bodies. Instead of bringing the food right to us, they unloaded the corn at a far distance and sent one messenger to tell us where to find the grain. Covering his nose with both hands, the messenger came running and shouting in the Ethiopian language of Amharic, but we could not understand him. Before we could figure out where the food was, the local people had taken it all. After a few hours, some of the boys heard the locals fighting over the maize, so they came to investigate. The locals beat the boys and drove them off. Swollen and bloody, they returned later to see what they could salvage. The lucky ones found a few grains, but most found nothing left. They roasted the maize in an open fire to make popcorn because there was too little to cook.

One day, after we had been in Funyido for three months, a white woman in a white Toyota arrived in our camp. Although she was traveling with other people, she was the one we will never forget. We watched in amazement as she alighted from the vehicle and exclaimed, "My God! My God!" several times before she burst into tears, shaking her head in disbelief. She stared at us starving, naked children, the dead bodies, and the vultures feeding on the carcasses, and she took many pictures with several different cameras.

Many of us became frightened because we had never seen such white skin and blue eyes. In our villages, we had seen babies with lighter skin and blue eyes, but their skin turned black and their eyes turned brown as they grew. This person was fully grown and had not darkened. We were also surprised that she did not cover her nose from the smell, as most people did. Some of us hoped this woman came to help us, but others became frightened that she was a dangerous animal or an enemy who wanted to kill us. We had never seen cameras before either, so we thought the strange objects were weapons like the ones the government troops had used against us in Sudan.

In all, the woman only stayed about ten minutes, taking pictures and talking rapidly on her radio. Her body was shaking as she spoke, and her face was filled with sympathy. We soon realized that she was not there to harm us. Those who were lying on the ground, weak and sick, lifted their heads up to see what was happening. After a short time, the woman climbed into her vehicle and drove away, leaving us wondering if she would be back. She had not been able to communicate with us because she did not know our language, but much later we found out that she worked for the United Nations office in Addis Ababa, the capital city of Ethiopia.

In less that a week, we were awakened at midnight by a rumbling noise that sounded like the military tanks we had heard in Sudan. In the distance, the lights of many vehicles flickered in the dark between the trees and bushes. Some of us began to worry that the white woman had betrayed us to our enemies who were sending tanks to kill us. As the noise approached, the youngest boys lost their hope that they would be rescued. Frantically, they searched for hiding places.

Soon the convoy arrived, but it passed by our camp, continued traveling down the road for about two miles, and stopped in an open spot for the night. We had never seen so many trucks—seventeen in all! After the last one faded into the night and the silence returned, we eventually stopped wondering what was in the trucks and went back to sleep on our dusty bedding.

The next morning, five workers from the Itang refugee camp arrived in a Toyota. When they began to speak to us in our own dialects, we could not believe our ears because most of us had come from the Upper Nile Region and from the Baralgazal tribes that had started the rebellion against the cruel government regime. The workers were shocked when they saw all the dead bodies and the filth. They could barely tell the difference between the dead and the living because flies covered everyone lying on the dusty ground. Their first order of business was to cook porridge for us because they knew we would not be able to swallow and digest solid food. Then they brought the trucks closer to the camp and began to distribute food, clothes, cooking utensils, blankets, and bath soap to us. We could not believe the items were ours to keep—we felt like we were stealing! We kept asking the workers questions during distribution: *Are these things mine? Can I take them with me? Will I use them and bring them back, or do I get to keep them?* After all our hardship, we were finally able to smile broadly again.

Looking like we had been painted because we were so dusty from sleeping on the dry ground, we all gladly went to the river to bathe with our soap and towels. When we were clean and dry, we put on our clean, new clothes, rejoicing in the generosity of our new friends. Then food was distributed to each group of boys. Some regrouping was needed because so many had fallen victim to starvation, disease, and enemies.

Two days later, when the first convoy of workers left, a team of the health workers arrived. The workers were not trained nurses, but they were able to read the English labels on the painkillers and medicines for dressing the wounds. Many boys were so ill that they still could not eat even though there was plenty of food available. Others were not able to walk because their leg wounds were infected. Measles was spreading through the camp, and there was no system of quarantine. The health workers discovered the measles and isolated the victims under different trees. The young boys felt shamed by their isolation, so teams of boys were posted to make sure the sick did not commit suicide as they counseled them not to be ashamed of their illness. The healthcare was inadequate, but the boys were far better off than they had been. Slowly, the camp was cleared of the stench of death as the workers buried the bodies, and the vultures and flies eventually abandoned the home of the Lost Boys to find other prey.

As the rainy season approached in April 1988, we had food and clothing, but we were still living under the trees. The United Nations workers returned to bring axes and other tools for us to use to cut trees and grass to build huts. We organized teams and divided the work: Some cut trees to make poles, others cut grass for thatch, and another group cooked food, hauled water, and cleaned up the camp. All the groups joined together to tie the poles together, to mud the walls, and to thatch the roofs. When the walls were half dry, a mixture of sandy soil and loamy soil was smeared inside and outside of the building so the walls would not crack in the heat of the day. We even built thirteen schools. We felt very proud of our work, but, unfortunately, we were not skilled builders. Later, some of our buildings collapsed and injured the boys inside, and most of our roofs leaked. Each year after the rainy season, we had to rebuild our homes and schools.

The camp did not have qualified teachers, but some older students who had been expelled by the Government of Sudan after the rebellion found their way to the camp during our second year in Ethiopia. These older students were able to teach us Arabic, mathematics, and a little English. Many of the Lost Boys had never attended school before, so we all gladly entered the first grade in 1987 in the Funyido Refugee Camp.

Some pencils and a few exercise books supplied by the United Nations were all we had for the thousands of students in the camp. We cut the books in half and the pencils into thirds. Each book half had twenty-four pages that were filled in and then erased so that others could use the book. The few teachers taught classes of two hundred or more boys for forty-five minutes while other students waited outside the building for their turns. School was in session during mornings and evenings, and we sat on the floor or stood in the back of the crowded schoolrooms. When we were not in class, we cooked, hauled water, and cleaned our huts. Several times a day some of us brought food for the teachers so that they could continue their lessons without stopping. The teachers worked for free until 1989, when the United Nations High Commissioner for Refugess (UNHCR) began to pay them ninety birr per month in Ethiopian money, which was equivalent to ten dollars in American money. Eventually, the UNHCR provided more books and textbooks, but we continued to share the exercise books.

Life was good for us for the next three years, from 1989–1991. The Ethiopian government welcomed us as refugees and protected us from abuse by the local people. The UNHCR continued to bring food and clothing, and they opened several clinics stocked with quality medicines. All these benefits made the local Anyuak people envious, so they occasionally attacked and robbed us of our food and clothing, especially when we were on our way home from the food distribution center.

Then, in 1990, the Anyuaks planned a massive attack. One afternoon at about three o'clock, a group of men armed with machine guns, knives, and other weapons invaded our camp, firing bullets into the crowded playground while other men, women, and children looted the huts. Twenty boys were killed, and many were wounded before the Ethiopian policemen arrived to help. The Ethiopian government tried to bring those responsible for the attack in to justice, but only a few people were convicted and sentenced to only two months in jail.

JOURNEY 3: FROM ETHIOPIA TO KENYA

In April 1991, our situation changed drastically when a rebellion overthrew the Ethiopian government and a new dictator took power. He immediately exiled all the officials and appointed his own. The new government did not want refugees in Ethiopia, so they began to destroy the camps and drive out the people. Eventually, the news reached us in Funyido that the Itang camp on the eastern border had been attacked and the government troops had killed many refugees and expelled the others. We Lost Boys were filled with fear; we had nowhere to go because new Sudanese refugees in our camp told us that the situation in Sudan was still hostile. We did not know what to do, so we waited.

One evening, several Ethiopian policemen who were loyal to the old government visited the Funyido camp to tell us that the new government was planning to attack our camp. The policemen urged us to leave within twenty-four hours because the rebels were not going to spare any lives. We had no choice but to begin planning another journey, so we decided that our only hope was to return to Pochalla where there were no Sudanese troops. Once again, we began looking for mosquito netting to protect ourselves during the coming rainy season.

In less than a week after the policemen warned us, we heard bombs and gunfire coming from the direction of Aboba as the new Ethiopian troops were trying to fight off the soldiers from the old government. There was no time to gather for prayer—we had to leave as soon as possible, so we grabbed all the supplies and grain we could carry and began walking along the Funyido River instead of crossing it because we feared that Ethiopian ground troops might find us before we would be able to cross to other side. We set out for Gilo, where we hoped to safely cross the river into Sudan once again. The flooded, narrow path led us southward into a forest. As we traveled through the thick bushes and tall grass, all of us were bitten mercilessly by the hungry mosquitoes, spiders, and scorpions, and some boys were even bitten—and killed—by poisonous snakes. When lions attacked us several times, the older boys tried to fight them off without weapons, but, again, they were unable to stop the beasts from killing some of the youngest boys.

Unfortunately, when the Ethiopian ground troops found the Funyido camp evacuated, they followed our trail. In the evening of the seventh day, we reached the Gilo area that was inhabited by a few Anyuak people. We built fires and boiled our maize in an open area near the river while a few older boys went to the local chief to ask him for boats to cross the river. Luckily, the chief sympathized with us and offered us one boat. Since night had already fallen when they returned with the boat, we had to wait until morning to cross the swift, deep river filled with crocodiles.

When dawn broke, the sick and youngest boys were taken across first in groups of ten. Those who knew how to swim did not even try because of the many crocodiles in the water. Once several of the vicious beasts tried to capsize a full boat. We thanked God that they did not succeed. We continued making slow trips back and forth across the river. By mid-afternoon, only about half of us were safely on the opposite bank when the soldiers finally caught up to the boys who were still waiting on the Ethiopian bank. No one saw the soldiers until they opened fire. The frightened boys had no other choice but to jump into the river full of crocodiles, even as the troops continued to shoot at them from the bank. That day, more than two thousand boys were killed by bullets, by crocodiles, and by drowning.

The swimmers who did reach the bank safely had nothing left but the clothes on their backs, but those of us who had crossed earlier gladly shared our food and blankets as we comforted them. Some were so very distressed over the loss of their friends that they had to be restrained from running away. Eventually, we set out to find Pochalla. The local people in Gilo had tried their best to give us directions, but none of us remembered where to go without a road or path to follow. We simply chose a direction and began trudging through flooded swamplands, sleeping on wet ground, and eating raw corn because we could not make fires in the rain.

Three days later, in May 1991, we finally found our way to Pochalla with the help of the local people. The weak and sick arrived the following day, but they did not get much rest because only two days later, the Sudanese government sent warplanes to bomb the town once again. Luckily, eleven of the twelve bombs missed their targets so only fifteen people were killed. Everyone fled and hid in the bushes about twenty miles from town.

Once again, we boys found ourselves living like animals without food to eat and shelter from the rain; we tried to keep warm with the few wet blankets we had left, and we began gathering wild fruit and leaves, but starvation and disease began to claim more lives. The local people in Pochalla had no doctor or clinic to help us.

The month of June finally brought relief when United

Nations representatives from Lokichioggio, Kenya, visited Pochalla and saw our plight. They brought staff from the International Committee of the Red Cross (ICRC) to help us with medicine and to prepare the field for deliveries from U.N. planes. On July 25, 1991, food and blankets arrived, so we thanked God for hearing our prayers again.

Life was better for several months, but our trials were not over. In October 1991, the Sudanese militia returned to attack the town, killing many when warplanes dropped bombs and ground troops invaded. We boys hid from the danger and planned another journey to find safety. At that time, fleeing to another country like Kenya was far from our minds. After being chased from Ethiopia and Pochalla, we realized that we would not be safe in any eastern African country, so we wanted to return to our homes in Sudan. Since we were all very homesick, the idea was appealing; we would rather die in our own villages with those we loved than in a foreign country with strangers, but we did not even know if our families were still alive because we had no way to contact them—we had never even seen a telephone. Finally, we admitted that going home was not possible, so we decided that we had better travel to Kenya instead.

Passing many abandoned towns, we walked for five months, covering thousands of miles across the desert, over mountains, and through bushes. Another deadly attack occurred in Mogus, where many more boys were killed by government troops, but the rest of us kept on. We settled for a time in Narus near the Kenyan border, where the United Nations found us and provided food and medicine, but when we heard that a nearby town, Kapoata, was under attack, we set out during the night toward Lokichioggio, a Kenyan town about one hundred miles away. When we arrived several days later, the United Nations brought water and food to us again as we camped west of town.

Unfortunately, the local Turkana people stole from us repeatedly, so in July 1992, we were moved by the United Nations to a new refugee camp in Kakuma, Kenya, which would become our home for many years. At first, the Kenyan tribes called us "Lost Kids" just as the Sudanese tribes had, but when American journalists visited the camp and heard our stories, they began to call us the Lost Boys of Sudan because they said we really were lost.

I was fourteen when I arrived in Kakuma, and my memories are still fresh. From 1994–1999, other refugees joined the camp as they, too, fled from violence in Ethiopia, Uganda, Congo, and Somalia. The Lost Boys were divided into seventeen groups with a minimum of eight hundred boys in each one. The camp was located in a dry desert with few trees that offered almost no shade for so many people. The United Nations provided tools and some materials, such as waterproof plastic sheeting for us to build huts, but we continued to cook our food over open fires. Sometimes, when the hot desert winds blew, the fires spread, burning our shelters to the ground. We had to rebuild them often.

Without knowing what we were doing, five of my young friends and I built our own hut. We put the plastic sheeting on the roof to keep out the rain, and we put grass over the sheeting to shield it from the sun. Unfortunately, the wind blew so strongly that all of the grass on our roof blew away within two months, and the plastic sheeting underneath melted in the hot sun. While we waited for our application for more building materials to be approved, we moved in with other friends who had built their roofs out of twigs that withstood the wind better than our grass. When the United Nations gave us more materials, we built our roof with twigs, too, so it lasted longer.

We were very happy to have a primitive clinic where we could get medicine for our diseases and injuries. However, it was poorly staffed, so those boys who were able to read the labels on the medicine bottles were allowed to give medicine and to dress the wounds of the other refugees. This was not the ideal situation, but it certainly shortened the waiting time for so many thousands of refugees who needed medical attention.

At that time, we did not know that 1992 would be the deadliest year ever in southern Sudan. Not only was the Sudanese government sending out its militia groups to kill Christians, but Osama Bin Laden, the leader of Al Qaeda, opened terrorists training camps in Sudan and commissioned his own militias to kill and destroy. The people in the south and the Sudan People's Liberation Army had no idea that Bin Laden was the world's most dangerous man until 2001, when he successfully orchestrated the bombing of the World Trade Center in New York City. They only knew that they were facing powerful Arab forces who carried keys in their pockets that would allow them to open a room in heaven full of beautiful virgins if they died for Allah in the name of Islam.

Other refugees told us similar stories of vicious fighting in our homeland. Every Saturday, the International Committee of the Red Cross (ICRC) brought wounded adults and children to Kakuma, so we had to settle them in our huts. These people shocked us with their stories about the killing going on in Sudan. They told us that they were lucky to only lose a leg or an arm before they were rescued by the Norwegian People's Aid (NPA)—the only relief organization that was still flying into the war zone after all the United Nations agencies stopped landing in southern towns.

Finding hiding places in southern Sudan was no longer easy because many members of the SPLA sold information to the government militias about the hiding places of villagers so that the soldiers raided and killed many. Extensive flooding in the south destroyed hiding places, and starvation, mosquitoes, snakes, and wild animals took many lives.

One man told us that he and many other men, women, and children were caught by the government troops. Almost all of the adults' hands were tied together with ropes so that no one in the group could escape. The two men who were not tied were then ordered to slaughter the children, to cook their bodies in a big drum, and to distribute the cooked flesh to the captives, who were forced to eat it at gunpoint. Finally, they were told to look up at the sky, to look to the left, the right, and back again. The soldiers said, "Now you have seen the world," and they opened fire on them. The soldiers thought they had killed everyone, but one man was only wounded in his jaw. After several hours, he regained consciousness, but he could not move because several dead bodies had fallen on him and his arms were still tied. As he prayed fervently, he slowly chewed through the blood-soaked ropes. He searched for other survivors among the thirty-seven bodies, but no one else was alive. He was able to make his way to the NPA, who brought him to safety in Kenya, but he could not eat for a week because he was repulsed by food that reminded him that he had eaten human flesh.

As he told us his story in Kakuma, we all began to cry. After that day, many of the Lost Boys stopped listening to others who escaped from southern Sudan because they could not stand the horrors. They were still trying to forget their own suffering, and they could not bear to hear any more. As more and more refugees fled from Sudan, we Lost Boys were convinced that they could not return to our homeland because it was too dangerous. We accepted our lives in Kenya and tried to make the best of our situation.

One bright spot during our stay was when the missionary from my village, Mark Nichols, moved to the refugee camp. When he came to Kakuma, he gained our trust because he could have lived with the white people, but he chose to live with us refugees. We realized that he was a true missionary who sincerely cared for us. Even when he was robbed and stabbed, he did not leave us. We were all amazed that he stayed in the camp and promised he would not leave us. He stayed as long as he could, but he was diagnosed with cancer in 2001 and moved to America in 2002, where he died.

When Nichols was with us, he really connected with the Lost Boys because we were interested in the Word of God. Some people used Christianity as a tool to rebel against the Muslims, but the Lost Boys really believed that Jesus was the true Son of God. We learned to read in the camps, so we began to read the Bible. Mark Nichols brought Dinka Bibles and preached in Dinka, but some chose to read English Bibles.

For many years the United Nations staff was faithful to deliver and distribute much-needed food to each refugee group twice a month, but the situation changed in 1997. The food deliveries were no longer regular, and we discovered that some of the U.N. authorities were corrupt when we went to the market in Kakuma and saw items for sale that had U.N. labels on them. We realized that someone was selling UN goods instead of giving them to the refugees.

After that, when our huts needed repairing, we were told that the United Nations was not able to distribute any more building materials. Even though some refugees were injured when their huts collapsed on them, they were told that they had to buy new building materials from the dealers who were friends of the U.N. officials in the shelter department. Many times, we saw trucks bring building materials to the U.N. compound, but they were not distributed; they were sold in the marketplace to anyone who had money to buy them. One pole cost 120.00 shillings in Kenyan money, which is equivalent to fifteen dollars in American money, but only a few refugees were able to work to have enough money for a single pole.

The food department was the most corrupt. In 1992, Mr. Kamau, a Kenyan, took charge of the food distribution. Soon he became known as Mr. Hyena because he preyed on the helpless. We learned that we would get nothing from him without a bribe. Some new arrivals told us that Kamau had previously worked in the U.N. immigration office in Lokichioggio, where he would only register refugees from Sudan who had money to pay him. Those who could not pay were ignored for two to three months until they could find a way to get money to bribe Kamau.

When Kamau came to Kakuma, he again refused to register refugees who could not pay him. Those who were not registered were not given ration cards, so their relatives had to share their food with them until they could figure out a way to pay for their registration. Kamau spent every weekend in Kakuma, selling—instead of giving—the UNCHR ration cards that were used as identification during food distribution. He sold a card that would feed five people for 3500.00 shillings, or fifty-five dollars. Kamau also sold U.N. food, such as cookies, to the refugees and the local people in several of his own food stores in Kakuma. We repeatedly reported these cases to the U.N. office, but nothing changed.

One day in 1998 I met some men from my tribe who had just fled the Sudan. They told me that my younger siblings, seven-year-old Emanuel, nine-year old Amer, and eleven-year-old Aja, were waiting for registration at the U.N. immigration office in Lokichioggio. Many of my friends gave me money so that I could take the bus to Lokichioggio. I was overjoyed to see them because I had not heard anything about my family since I left my village in 1987, but I wept when they told me that my parents and many other siblings were dead.

I found that Mr. Kamau had not registered my brother and sisters because they did not have money to bribe him. I walked to Mr. Kamau's office and asked him the reason he could not register my siblings. He told me that the U.N. office in Kakuma had not supplied him with enough office equipment. He asked me in the Kiswahili language, "Tua kitu kidogo," which means "remove something small." He meant that I needed to pay him if I wanted to register my relatives, so I gave him 700.00 Kenyan money, equivalent to ten dollars. He was so excited that he registered them and me with double rations, even though he knew I already had rations because I came from Kakuma. He also made sure that we were the first ones given seats in the trucks headed back to Kakuma that day. Those people who could not afford to pay were left behind for two months or more.

When we returned to the camp, my sisters were not able to live with me in the boys' section of the camp, so my brother, four of my friends, and I moved to the co-ed area, Zone 3. My friends and I built three huts for the ten of us.

At this time, I was scheduled to be resettled in the United States with other Lost Boys, but I could not leave my sisters behind. My fears were very real because unprotected girls were often raped or forced into marriage at an early age. I had seen young orphan girls taken in broad daylight to be sold for "wives," but they really became slaves. Some had to fetch water, cook, and perform all the heavy chores for their households, and they were not allowed to attend school. I could not allow that to happen to my sisters who had already suffered for so long during the war; therefore, I decided to cancel my case with the Immigration and Naturalization Service (INS). I dreaded the idea of letting my friends go to America without me, but I knew that my sisters needed me and that I would never see them again if I left.

In 2000, I was again told that I was scheduled to be resettled in the United States of America. I had grown up in a small village without television or radio, so I knew nothing about Western countries except the rumors I had heard. I had heard that America was a country where green cards were given to foreigners as documents to get a little food but that immigrants were not allowed to become permanent residents. I believed that I would have to work every day for only a few coins for transportation because the government would take all my money. I was afraid because I heard that people were shot while walking on streets in the United States of America. Since many of the Lost Boys thought that America was a dangerous country, they refused to be resettled there, and others did not want to go to other countries because they feared traveling anywhere. They had suffered so much during their journey to Ethiopia, back to Sudan, and into Kenya in 1992 that they feared leaving again. Less than half of the Lost Boys agreed to register in 1998 to be resettled to a foreign country.

However, some who did leave Kenya for the United States began to send letters, photographs, and even money back to their friends in Kakuma in 2000. We could not believe what they told us. They described America as a second heaven filled with food, money, schools, and people who love them. The photos showed the beauty and the wealth of America. Some boys took photos of each other lying on green grass outside their apartments. We saw pictures of boys in kitchens, holding fruit and vegetables as they sat next to freezers. We saw them lying on big mattresses in their own bedrooms. Those who attended school sent photos of themselves with their white friends, and others showed them eating at beautiful tables with white families who adopted them.

The resettled boys also praised the justice system in America. One Lost Boy named Kuei in Michigan wrote that the militia who had slaughtered his father and brother would have been severely punished if they had committed their crimes in America where the police are not corrupt. One day when Kuei was only four years old, he was returning home with his father and his sixteen-year-old brother when militiamen stopped them. His father was carrying Kuei on his shoulder, so the soldiers ordered him to put the boy down. As Kuei watched in horror, the men forced his father and brother to the ground and shot them in cold blood. Luckily, some of the men convinced the others to spare the little boy. They kept Kuei with them for a few hours until they found a woman and ordered her to take him. The woman recognized Kuei because they were from the same clan, so she returned the boy to his mother. Kuei was too young and scared to tell them exactly what had happened, but the blood spatter on his body told enough of the story.

All this information convinced many people that they were wrong about America. Those who had turned down registrations were especially sad that they had been mistaken about such a wonderful country. But others could not believe what they saw in the photos, claiming that the photos were fakes and that the food and vegetables were only toys. They said the boys eating at tables with white people must be in restaurants, not the homes they live in. I was somewhat confused, too, because one of my friends sent me a letter describing his car, a 1999 Ford, and I thought he was lying because I could not understand how he could have his own car when he had only been in America for two months.

This misconception of life in America caused many problems for us in the Kakuma camp in Kenya. Throughout our experiences, we Lost Boys had fought to survive. No matter how bad the situation, no one had despaired, but when the boys who had relocated in America began writing about the wealth and safety they found in America, many who had refused resettlement lost hope. Within the first two months of communication between the Lost Boys in America and those in Kenya, five boys hung themselves. Only one left a suicide note addressed to his friend, explaining that he will meet him again in heaven because life on earth was too difficult to face. More suicide attempts followed, as well as other problems. Some boys dropped out of the Kakuma schools and began drinking to find the happiness that they had been seeking since the war had begun. Drinking gave them only temporary relief because they began fighting with each other, losing the friendships that had grown during their struggles.

The Lost Boys in America were burdened to encourage their African friends, so they began sending money each month, hoping to prevent more suicides. I believe the Lost Boys in America have sent more money back to their homeland than any other immigrant group in America. Additional funds were sent at Christmas because the custom in Africa is to celebrate by buying new clothing and feasting, so people feel ashamed if they are poor and stay inside their homes to avoid being seen in their old clothing. Americans who eat good food all year long might not understand the importance of feasting at Christmas in Africa, where people live on corn all year and look forward to eating chicken and other special foods to celebrate Christ's birth.

Even today, in 2005, many Lost Boys in Africa who have completed high school are looking for funds from their friends in the U.S. so that they can finish their education or relocate to other countries. Some countries, like Australia, accept refugees, but they do not pay their expenses. Refugees must pay for resettlement applications, medical check-ups, and airplane tickets. The Lost Boys in America are the only hope the Africans have for new lives, and we give gladly to show our love, just as God has blessed us. Even though we are not blood relatives, God has given us each other to care for and to love for over fifteen years—in war and in peace.

Unfortunately, some of the refugees in Kakuma have little hope of resettlement because the U.N. staff in Kakuma sold their identities to refugees from other countries that had money to bribe the officials. Not all refugees are poor; wealthy people come to Kakuma seeking safety from civil wars in many different countries such as Somalia, Rwanda, Uganda, Ethiopia, Congo, and Zaire. While the real boys were waiting for their interviews with the Joint Voluntary Agency (JVA) and the Immigration and Naturalization Service, one of the UNHCR representatives for the Lost Boys sold their files to other refugees who had money. When the names were called, two people showed up for the interview, so the cases were rejected by INS and sent to the UNHCR for investigation. The files were hidden, so the authorities could not find out what had happened. In all, 505 files for boys who had registered for resettlement never showed up until the interview process ended.

Five other boys were rejected during interviews because the JVA team leader was given a note claiming that they were not the right people. Their case was also sent to the United Nations, but nothing was done even though they were the right people with the correct names. One of the five boys committed suicide when he realized that he would not be resettled.

JOURNEY 4: FROM KENYA TO AMERICA

Finally, in 2001, I decided that I should apply for resettlement again because the good news about America was driving me crazy. I went to the U.N. resettlement office in Kakuma. I asked the guard if I could get a resettlement application. The guard led the way to the office where, once again, I was face to face with Mr. Kamau, the man I had to bribe to get my sisters registered with the United Nations. He was now working for the UNHCR. I explained to him why I had canceled my previous resettlement and told him that I was now ready to leave. Mr. Kamau laughed as he pointed his finger at me and told me I was stupid. Then he told me that he could help me to travel to Australia, Canada, or the United States of America, but that he needed money to talk with people he knew on the U.N. staff in Kakuma or in Nairobi. When I asked how much money he needed, he asked me how many people I wanted to take with me to America. He said that each of us would cost forty thousand shillings, which is equivalent to five hundred dollars. That meant I would have to pay him $3,500.00 for the seven of us. I had never even seen so much money! He said that he could not trust us to pay him later because he had helped other refugees who had agreed to send him one thousand dollars, but they never did after they arrived in America. He swore that he would not help any others unless they paid him some money first.

I was upset by his demands, so I walked out without a word.

Later, I decided that I would try to find someone else to help me. Going to Mr. Kamau's superiors at the INS or approaching the Joint Volunteer Agency (JVA) in Kakuma would be useless because they would protect Mr. Kamau, so I decided to travel to Nairobi where the INS and JVA district offices were located.

Little did I know the trouble that waited for me. Nairobi is a big city that I had never been to before, and I did not know anyone who lived there. When I arrived, I was dirty from the bus ride, so people must have thought I was a thief because they ran away when I approached them to ask directions. Without enough money for lodging, I spent the first night in the bus station. The next day, I tried to ask people where the US Embassy was, but they would not answer and moved their luggage closer to them when I came near. I wanted to contact some of the Lost Boys in America to help me, but I had no way to reach them. Finally, on the third day in the bus station, I met one southern Sudanese who was living in Nairobi, and I explained my situation and asked if he would take me with him to his place so that I could finally shower and eat. He said I could stay with him while I tried to find someone to help me with my resettlement.

Two days later, I asked him if he could show me the U.S. Embassy in Nairobi. He took me right away to Gigiri, where the embassy is located. However, the guards drove me away immediately before they even heard what I had to say. They must have thought I was a criminal by the way I was dressed.

A week later, the man I was living with bought a phone card to call my friends in the U.S. Because of all we have been through together, we Lost Boys of Sudan love each other more than we love our relatives. We believe that God gave us to each other for support during our struggles as refugees, so the boys I contacted were eager to help me. Within three days, two of my friends in Boston sent three hundred dollars. I was thrilled to get so much money! I hired a homeless man for fifty cents to take me to the JVA Office in Westland in Nairobi. Unfortunately, those guards also drove me away.

I was getting desperate because I was worried about my relatives alone in the camp in Kakuma. I prayed to God for help, specifically asking Him for help in our resettlement. I prayed each day before I went out to find help. Some days I was very upset with myself for canceling my first resettlement, but I knew that regrets would not help me now. Many times I got lost in the city as I searched for someone to help me. One day I went to the International Organization of Migration (IOM). I was not driven away as usual, but no one let me in to meet an official. I spent three hours standing next to the IOM gate. I tried to make friends with the Kenyan men who passed by, but they were not interested in my friendship and simply walked by. I felt all alone in the world.

Then I met Alice Juan. I was walking away from the IOM building to the bus stop when a woman walking behind me called out for me to wait for her. I stopped suddenly, hoping she was calling from inside the IOM compound. She was a beautiful woman, so I was surprised that she just wanted to talk to me. She introduced herself as Alice and asked which Kenyan tribe I belonged to; I replied that I am Sudanese, not Kenyan. She wanted us to walk side by side while we talked, but I could not make myself walk alongside such a wonderful woman. I walked behind her so that she could not see me as she asked me several questions about my country. Then she asked what I wanted in Nairobi. I told her about my quest for resettlement to America, so she told me that she, too, was looking for a visa to travel to Europe for her studies.

As we visited, Alice and I climbed into the same bus to travel downtown. She began singing gospel songs and smiling to herself. I could see tears rolling down her cheeks, and she told me that she would pay my bus fare. Stepping off the bus, I thanked her, but before I could take another step, she again called for me to stop. She took my hands and asked me to pray with her right there on the busy sidewalk. Surprised, I agreed, but I did not trust her. As soon as she started praying, I opened my eyes because I thought she must be a criminal who had friends nearby who would kill me when my eyes were closed. She was holding my fingers very tightly, so I looked around for any suspicious people who might be approaching while she was praying. After Alice finished praying, she kissed my hands, gave me her contact information, and told me to call her the next afternoon. On my way home, I told myself that this woman was either mentally ill or a fool because she kissed my dirty hands.

The following morning I called her to hear what she wanted me to do. She said that I should wait for her for about fifteen minutes in a certain building located in the Nairobi city center. She arrived in less than ten minutes and asked me to walk with her to the Nairobi Cinema, a big church that holds a prayer meeting during the lunch hour at twelve o'clock noon every day. She asked me to sit in the lobby and pray with her before the church service started, and she said that God had told her to help me before we had even met the day before. After the church service, she suggested that we should both go to the UNHCR in Nairobi to apply for a U.N. passport to America. She told me that I should pray while she talked to the officials. After we boarded the bus, I asked her how many passports the United Nations would give to me because I need to take my siblings with me to America. Since the United Nations would only give me one passport, she canceled the trip and told me she would think of something else.

We met in the Nairobi Cinema for prayers again the next day. She surprised me when she said that God had showed her that I was not interested in her help. She asked me to commit myself to the mission God gave her. I told her that I was interested in what she was doing for me, but, in reality, I was still worried that she might be a criminal pretending to be nice in order to rob me. In Kakuma, I had been warned that women like that style of crime, so I could not trust her completely.

In Nairobi, there was a small Sudanese church where people pray every Saturday. I approached the senior pastor, Paul Deng, and told him how I had met Alice and how she was trying to help me. Then I asked him if God would send a Kenyan woman to help me in such a way because I was afraid that she was a criminal who wanted to kill me. Pastor Deng laughed as he told me that God's work is very wide and complex. He believed it was a work of God to send Alice and that he did not believe she was a criminal because no thief would use her own money for a person like me who had no property of his own.

Even though Pastor Deng had relieved some of my fears, I was not interested in meeting Alice again because I had never known anyone who claimed to hear so much from God. I thought she was lying when she told me that God had told her that I was not interested in her help because she could probably tell that just from the way I acted toward her.

On the day we had agreed to meet, I called Alice to say that I could not go to the church because I did not have bus fare. She asked me whose phone I was using, so I told her I was calling from a Kenyan man's shop. She asked me to give the receiver to the owner of the shop, and she told him that she would repay him if he would lend me some money for the bus.

The shop owner was so suspicious that he asked me to give him my ID and address because he thought I was criminal who had coordinated the deal with the woman. When I explained the situation, the man gave me the money and said I did not have to repay him, but he was glad later when I came back with his money.

At the church, as Alice and I waited for the prayer meeting to start, she asked me where I wanted to be resettled. I replied that I wanted to go to the United States, Canada, or Australia. Then she told me that God wanted me to read certain Bible verses, and she assured me that I would be sent to the United States in the fall. Alice told me that God answers her prayers, and she told me a story to prove it.

Once, when Alice's boss wanted to fire her because he wanted to hire his own relative, she prayed that God would only let her boss fire her if she did not have a pure heart. She prayed that her boss would not fire her if she was serving God's people the way that He wanted her to. When she went to the office the next day, her boss told her that she could keep her job. However, her story only half convinced me that I would be resettled so soon because I had not even applied yet.

The following morning, I decided to go to IOM. When the guard was not looking, I was able to sneak in the building. An American man from Boston met me, typed my application, and sent it to the INS office in Nairobi. I left that building filled with joy. God had answered my prayers at last!

After three months in Nairobi, I was finally able to return to my relatives in Kakuma to await news from the INS. I was anxious to see if they were safe because I knew that the local people were armed with AK-47 rifles. They would often loot the refugee camps at night, looking for food and killing refugees who tried to stop them. We did not even try to lock our huts because we were safer if we just let the robbers take what they wanted. They claimed that the United Nations had been supplying them with food before refugees came to Kakuma. Now they said their share was being given to new settlers instead of to them.

In 2001, a boy named Aloung was killed one week before he was to leave for a new life in America. He had invited his friends to meet in his hut at seven o'clock p.m. to celebrate his resettlement. As Aloung and his friends listened to music and ate, five gunmen heard the radio and came to take it, along with any food they could find. Aloung was killed because he was standing by the door, singing and offering food and drink to his guests. Everybody who knew him mourned the loss of such an honest and wise friend who had been one of the encouragers during the trip of the Lost Boys. When he was only nine years old, Aloung had given us hope by telling us that God is not a murderer who would kill all the children of the same generation in one day. He said that some of us would die but that some would live long, good lives. His words are still remembered by the Lost Boys who have reached the United States of America.

After I returned from Nairobi, I was afraid that I would be killed just like Aloung had been. When a friend and I were sitting beside the fire outside his hut, some armed men approached us, shot bullets into the fire, and told us they wanted our possessions. They took our towels, clothes, and shoes, but they did not hurt us. I was very thankful that my life was spared.

Many of us in the camp believed that policemen brought by the United Nations were responsible for many killings because one night gunmen looting in Zone 3 shot one of their colleagues after they mistook him for a villager when he was leaving one of the huts. The man was found the following morning with a gun wound in his chest, and he was identified as the Kenyan police officer who was responsible for the refugees' night curfew. The camp officials took him to the United Nations representatives for further investigation, and they determined that the top police officer had shot him. The community was shocked when they heard the report.

The lack of trustworthy law enforcement caused other problems too. The Lost Boys in the camp lived in fear of the Turkana people of Kenya who are very primitive; the women wear animal skins and the men go naked. The Turkana resented the presence of refugees in their district because they assumed that the Lost Boys were going to settle permanently in their land, and they also believed that the U.N. supplies that were given to the refugees were supposed to be given to them. Therefore, the Turkana attacked, killed, and looted the Sudanese at gunpoint, and they raped the women who left the camp to gather firewood. To protect my sisters, I would not let them leave the camp, so I gathered our firewood by myself.

We also had medical problems in the camp. The U.N. "hospital" left much to be desired because there were no medical doctors in the facility, and patients with serious illnesses could only be transferred to Nairobi if bribes were given to the officials who made the schedule. The local people had money for bribes, but the refugee patients without money sometimes died before they were transferred. When one of my friends was admitted, I was the one who had to take care of him because the nurses did little except dispense medication. When I saw that patients were sharing beds, mattresses, and blankets because the U.N. workers had sold the hospital supplies in the market, I brought bedding from home so my friend could be comfortable. Fortunately, he was discharged from the hospital in one week.

Corruption also affected the distribution of ration cards. Every two years, officials conducted a headcount to renew ration cards. White officials from Nairobi and New York supervised the centers during the headcounts, but they did not know that African and Middle Eastern U.N. workers secretly sold extra cards to refugees with money. I knew people who bought more than fifty cards because they had a lot of cash, so in one of the headcounts, I bought thirteen ration cards in addition to our actual cards. I knew it was a serious crime to buy cards, but I felt I had to because our rations were being reduced after the U.N. staff found out that some people had gotten extra cards.

Often the food that was distributed to us did not last until the next distribution. Every two weeks three kilograms of corn was distributed to each person, but we had to trade some of it for firewood, beans, and salt because the United Nations rarely gave us those items. When we ran out of corn, we called those days "black days" because we were so hungry. The few who had money were able to buy food from the market, but the poorer refugees lived without anything to eat. In contrast to the black days, we also had what we called "white men dust" times that were happy days for us refugees because the white inspectors came to Kakuma to oversee the food distribution to the refugees and every U.N. worker ran to open all the food stores to distribute food in large quantities. At these times we received items that were not given otherwise, such as beans, salt, cooking oil, and even firewood so that the visitors would think we had what we needed. The bad news about the "white man dust" days was that the visitors only came once a year.

After I finished the process to have my sisters resettled with me in the United States of America, a series of events occurred that made me very glad that I stayed to protect my young sisters. I began to notice that some refugees had begun to treat me unkindly. I did not understand why, so I simply avoided them. One day two elders came to my home and tried to convince me that girls cause a lot of trouble in America, so I should leave my sisters behind with them and travel to the United States of America alone. I politely rejected their suggestion by saying that I was ready to face any problem the girls might cause in the future. They walked out without even saying good-bye. A short time later some of my friends told me that they had heard of a plan to kidnap my sisters and take them back into Sudan to sell. My friends warned me to be very careful to keep the secret and to protect the girls.

I was grateful for their advice, but I decided that I had to tell my sisters and the authorities, so the following morning I reported the rumor to the U.N. security office. The officer told me that I could take my sisters to a special protection area in the camp until it was time to fly to America, but I did not want to take the girls there because I knew that the U.N. staff members and the Kenyan police often raped women if they refused to have sex with them. I had seen women inside the fence crying for help after being attacked by the guards, and many women refused to stay in the "protection" area because they said it was better to be forced into a marriage than to be raped. I was also afraid that my sisters might be tricked into a bad relationship. Sometimes U.N. staff members stole clothes and food from the U.N. stores to bribe attractive women living outside the protection area to leave their husbands and families and to live with them, so the divorce rate increased and families were broken. Eventually, some of the staff abandoned the women if they became pregnant because they did not want the burden of a family.

Another example of the power of the corrupt police in Kenya really frightened me. One of my cousins had a beautiful girlfriend who caught the eye of a Kenyan policeman. When she refused his advances, the man became so angry that he set out to kill my cousin and take the girl. The man searched parties, bars, and streets, looking for my cousin before he left to be resettled in Australia. Finally, the girl gave in to the policeman to save the life of her boyfriend, the father of her child. She took her little boy and moved in with the policeman. My cousin had no one to turn to for help because the authorities taking the complaints were the same ones committing the crimes.

I did not want my sisters to suffer such a fate, so, refusing the offer of the protection area, I walked to the UNHCR compound to ask for permission to travel to Nairobi to wait for our flight to America. I arrived at three o'clock p.m., but I could not see a staff member without money to bribe the guards. Since the office closed at four o'clock, I begged them to let me in because I had to travel back home that day to protect my sisters, but they refused to let me in to see the white woman who was the protection officer for the camp. Returning the next morning, I brought fifty shillings to bribe the guards, so I was allowed in, but no one seemed willing to help me. I explained to one official, Mr. Johnson, that I needed to travel to Nairobi for safety, but he did not tell me what to do next.

Confused, I simply sat on the bench inside the compound because I did not want to have to bribe the guards to get back in. I was not allowed to speak to the protection officer, so I was still sitting there at four o'clock. I had come at eight a.m. and had not eaten all day, so I finally had to leave the U.N. compound to find food and water. As I rode my bicycle and wondered what to do next, I noticed that Mr. Johnson was following me in his car. He pulled alongside of me and asked if I had five hundred shillings to give him to produce the traveling document right away. I had seen U.N. corruption before, but

I had not known that I would have to "buy" my travel documents. I told him that I had money, so he immediately turned his car around and headed back to the U.N. compound, and I followed on my bicycle. He told the guards to stop me at the gate, but he went inside to print the document because it was already five p.m. so the rest of the staff had gone home. When he returned to me, he told me I needed to get a passport photo taken somewhere else because the U.N. camera was locked inside the office of the protection officer. He drove me to a studio in Ethiopia to get the photo taken. I paid him the money, he placed the stamps on my new passport, and I was ready to travel. He warned me that the serial number in the document was invalid, so if I got caught, I should mention his name. I kept that document with me when I came to America, so I have proof of U.N. corruption because the wrong card numbers and serial numbers do not match my UNHCR registration cards.

Night was coming, so I had no time to waste. I bribed a policeman with another five hundred shillings to drive me back to my family and then to take all of us to the bus station. We took some bedding and some clothes, but we left most of our belongings behind. Nobody asked where I was going because the policeman was still with me. I said good-bye to my friends, and we drove five miles to the bus station. I did not have enough bus fare to get us to Nairobi, so we traveled for half the day and got off at the town of Nakuru.

It was already night, so I had to find a safe place for us to sleep. We all had to stay in one bedroom because I could not afford more rooms. Early in the morning, I left my siblings in the room to find a house quickly because checkout time was nine a.m. I looked in the slums and found a cheap place to live for 150.00 shillings, which is two dollars a month per room.

The best I could find was in the Shabbab slum. The place was hardly livable, but we had no choice. The floors were dirt, the rooms smelled like alcohol, a board was used as the door, and the windows were covered by rags so the insects were thick inside. It did not have running water or electricity, and I had to kill the cockroaches and take the fireplace ashes to the garbage. I picked up my relatives from the hotel, and we moved into the house. We bought water for drinking, cooking, and washing. Without a bathroom, we took showers outside in the dark night. We had to put a heavy rock by the door to keep the wind from blowing it in on us.

The nights were terrifying because we were afraid of thieves and loud noises. Sometimes we were awakened by drunks throwing rocks on our roof made of corrugated iron sheets. That sound was louder than a gunshot. We did not speak the same dialect that our neighbors spoke, so we could not communicate with them. Our bedding became very dusty as we slept on the hard-packed dirt floor without beds or chairs. We used the little money we had wisely for the first week, but then I had to leave my siblings behind and travel to Nairobi to ask my friends in America to send me more money and to contact the UNHCR staff in Nairobi.

When I arrived at the U.N. office, I reported my case to one of the caseworkers, and I was told they would not look into my problem unless they heard a report from the U.N. office in Kakuma. I did not want to waste my time because I wanted to get back to protect my family, so I went to the International Organization for Migration (IOM) for assistance where I met Sasha Chanoff, a thirty-year-old white man from Boston who was working for the IOM. After I explained my problems to him, he became angry and felt sorry for what had happened to us. Without hesitation, he e-mailed the US Embassy and gave me some money from his own pocket to rescue my siblings. I returned to Nakuru with the promise that Chanoff would let me know as soon as he heard from the US Embassy.

I was happy to find my siblings were safe. One week later I called Chanoff and heard good news. He had met with a white woman named Elizabeth who was working as a coordinator for Joint Volunteer Agency (JVA) in Nairobi. She was alarmed by our situation, so she ordered us to be moved to a protection shelter in Nairobi. Although conditions there were not the best, we were better off than we had been in Shabbab because there was maximum security. We waited in the shelter from June 28, 2003, to the day we flew to America in September 2003.

After the terrorist attacks on the World Trade Center buildings on September 11, 2001, I worried that U.S. Immigration would shut down the resettlement program so we would not be allowed into America. My fear was fueled when I witnessed U.N. staff members selling forms for money to non-refugees instead of giving them to registered refugees. I was afraid that terrorists would get to America through the U.N., causing the U.S. Government to pull out of the United Nations. I had also seen an Arabic man on a bicycle drop a pouch one evening. Bystanders called for him to stop, but he fled in fear. When the bag was opened, we saw it was full of passports from Jordan, Kenya, Saudi Arabia, and Iran. The bag was taken to the UNHCR office, but no arrest was ever made.

Despite my fears, my siblings and I successfully finished the INS interviews, the medical examinations, and the orientation into American culture with the US Embassy in 2002. We were scheduled for resettlement in the fall, just as Alice Juan had predicted.

Before I left Africa, I wanted one last look at Sudan, so on

June 14, 2003, I returned to my homeland after living in exile for sixteen years. I wanted to investigate the rumors I had heard in the Kakuma Refugee Camp that another one of my stepsisters had been wandering alone in Sudan after her mother and siblings had died from starvation in 1999. I was horrified by the thought that nobody was taking care of her, and I wanted to find her and help her before I left the continent. I received permission and a free round-trip ticket to travel to Panyagoor, which is a small town near my homeland in the Upper Nile Region that was controlled by the Sudanese Sudan People's Liberation Army (SPLA).

After I arrived in Panyagoor, I began the 115-mile walk northward to my hometown, Duk-payuel. Since I was only ten years old when I had left Sudan in 1987, I did not know the way home, so I joined a group of women who were also traveling to that region. To protect me, they advised me to walk in my underwear and to carry my clothes in a pouch. That way, if I met the militia, the men would not kill me for my clothes. The women also told me that I should walk with my back hunched over so that my tall frame could not be seen from a distance. As we walked for two days, I saw many abandoned villages littered with human bones. I remembered the people I had seen living there years before, and I became very sad and fearful. On the third day, we arrived in Duk-payuel.

I searched in six surrounding villages, asking everyone I met if they had any news about the families of the Lost Boys. I was shocked when the surviving villagers told me how many had died from starvation, disease, and government killings. The survivors took care of the orphans as much as possible. Only two mothers of my friends were still alive, but all their sisters, brothers, and fathers were dead. When I told the mothers that their boys were still alive, they could not believe their ears. They started singing gospel songs of praise, and they told me to tell their sons that their mothers loved them very much. I found some of my distant relatives among the disabled adults and orphaned children, but no one could tell me where I could find the remains of my parents. I found many dried bones that could not be identified. I felt terrible when people asked me if I knew what had happened to their sons who were Lost Boys because I had seen many of them killed on the journey to Ethiopia. Sometimes I pretended that I did not know what had happened to their boys because I was afraid that they would be too upset by the news. All the villagers were very happy that I had returned, and they said it was a miracle to hear the news that many of the Lost Boys were still alive.

Mr. Mabil, the head of the local chiefs, told me that there were about twenty-three different militia groups that were being financed and supplied with ammunition by the Government of Sudan. The soldiers from one militia camp located fifty miles from Jolong made life unbearable for the natives because the soldiers intercepted U.N. supplies that the people need to survive. Also, if the natives planted crops, the soldiers let their own cattle graze on the seedlings in the farmers' fields. The farmers were shot if they tried to drive the cattle away. Some of the young native girls offered themselves to the soldiers as sex slaves because the militia camps had food from looting and from the government. Many of the natives would have liked to leave, but they could not because the healthy ones wanted to stay to take care of all the young orphans and the disabled who were not able to walk out of the country.

I was also told that the militia leaders kept women captive who had been kidnapped from villages, especially young girls ages twelve to fifteen years old. I was devastated to learn that my stepsister was among twenty-seven women under the con-

trol of one commander. The chief warned me not to attempt
to go beyond the village to rescue her because I might be killed.
The chief moved me from place to place because he feared that
someone would betray him to the militia to keep me from
helping my stepsister.

The chief told me that Christians were still being killed
and that churches were bombed to kill the pastors. Three days
before I arrived, a pastor was killed in his hut during the night
because he preached the Word of God to villagers in an open
place. The militia had spies in the village who betrayed anyone who broke the government regulations. The first regula-
tion was that no meeting or group of five people could gather
without permission from the militia authorities so that they
could monitor what was said at the meeting. In some places
where the militia was based, churches were closed because the
militia attacked the worship service. If no public prayers were
held, militia spies were still able to turn in the church leaders
and pastors to be killed. Spies were paid with food, so desperate people betrayed their neighbors. The Government of Sudan
had created the proverbial "dog eat dog" culture of survival.

The most upsetting conversation I had with the chief and
villagers occurred when I told them that I was going to live in
America. They asked me if I wanted to have children some-
day because they had been told that America does not want
people to have sex so that they will not have children. Because
the villagers were primitive and illiterate, they had no way
of learning what was happening in the world around them,
so they believed whatever the government agents told them.
The agents were able to convince them that AIDS stands for
"American Ideologists Discourage Sex," and that it is a con-
spiracy to prevent overpopulation. I felt sad when I realized
that the government wanted the people to remain ignorant so

that the AIDS virus could infect them and kill them all. The villagers were surprised when I told them that AIDS is a deadly disease that is killing millions of people around the world and that the government wanted to kill them by letting the disease spread. The chief and the villagers told me that I should leave as soon as possible before the militia found out that I was spreading the truth about AIDS.

Before I left, I recognized two orphaned boys because they looked like one of my close friends, Joseph Nyok, so I knew they were his brothers. Joseph and I had shared good and bad times during our journey as Lost Boys before he died from an unknown disease in 1991 when we were walking to Kenya. He had told me about his family, but I had never met them. Naked and homeless, Deng and Simon Manyoun were only twelve and fourteen years old, so finding food on their own was hard. The rest of their family had died from cholera.

Because the boys did not know me, I introduced myself to them and told them that I had known their brother. I also had to tell them that Joseph was dead. I felt so sorry for them that I decided I would assume Joseph's role as their older brother and take responsibility for them. On my fourth day in southern Sudan, all three of us walked back to Panyagoor and boarded the plane to fly to Kenya and the Kakuma Refugee Camp.

The lives of the boys improved greatly in the camp. I bought them clothes with the little money I had, and I planned to bring them with me to America. Unfortunately, my processes were completed so that my siblings and I were only waiting for a flight to North Dakota. The American Embassy would not place them in my file, so I had to leave them behind in the camp when we left for America.

Finally, on September 10, 2003, Adual, Jacob, Ajueny, Aja, Amer, Emanuel, and I flew into Fargo, North Dakota.

We were surprised and overjoyed to hear my name shouted in the terminal by workers from our sponsoring organization, Lutheran Social Services (LSS). They greeted us with flowers and money, and they helped us get settled in our own apartment in a strange, cold land. We were safe from harm, but not safe from struggles.

My first three months of adjusting to such a new culture were quite challenging. Having lived only in grass huts, I did not know how to live in such a nice home. My bed had always been the hard ground, so I could not sleep on a soft mattress because I felt as if I was in the air and falling down. For the first three months in America, I slept on the floor until I adjusted to the feeling of the bed. Making meals was another problem because the only foods I could find that I knew how to cook were rice and chicken.

We were not alone, though, because several families volunteered to help us, and I soon learned that American women are honest and sincere because they treated us as if we were their own children. One other Lost Boy had told me that ninety percent of the possessions and advice given to refugees has come from American women, and I experienced that firsthand because we were given many wonderful items, such as furniture, a TV, and a washing machine. At first, I was fearful that they would want the items returned to them or that I would have to pay to replace them if we broke them, because those are the customs in some African communities. I was very relieved to learn that the gifts were mine to keep.

My sisters and brother were quickly registered for school, and since I had graduated from the United Nations school in Kenya, I wanted to go to college, but I did not really consider it for several reasons: (1) I had to get a job to support us, (2) my English was hard for others to understand, (3) I thought I was too old, (4) I had no way to pay for an education, and (5) I did not know who would supervise my siblings if I worked full time while going to school. Going to college seemed impossible until I prayed and God answered. I passed the college entrance test, I qualified for financial aid, and all the other problems were solved too. I was admitted to North Dakota State University and began working toward a degree in Criminal Justice.

When I began my first job, I felt suspicious when I realized $150 was taken out of each check for taxes. I thought the government was taking advantage of me, so I asked one of my white co-workers if I could see his check. He did not want to show me at first, but I kept asking because I did not realize that people in America do not like to talk about their income. He finally asked me why I wanted to see it and showed me that he pays twice as much in taxes as I do. I was surprised that a third-generation American has to pay so much to the government. My first income tax return was a very fearful experience for me too. My refund was so large that I worried I had not filled out the forms correctly. I hoped that I would not get in trouble with the government for unintentional tax fraud.

Soon after I arrived, I found out that the person I had asked to take care of Deng and Simon Manyoun back in Kenya was abusing them and making them work instead of letting them go to school. Also, their U.N. ration cards had been taken away from them, so they were suffering. I was so sad when I heard how badly they were treated that I decided to send them to a boarding school in Kenya were they would be safe and where they could prepare themselves for future work by getting an education. Since I was working, I began sending $250.00 a month to pay for their school fees, boarding fees, and other supplies. I feel very glad that I am able to help the brothers of my friend.

Going to school and working full time was not easy when I started. LSS had given me a car, but it broke down during the first week of college. I rode a bicycle until winter came, and then I had to take the bus. Waiting for the bus in the cold North Dakota weather was hard for me, but that was the only way I could get to the grocery store, to work, and to school since I had nothing in the bank to buy a car. I considered quitting school because I missed a lot of classes.

Eventually, a friend helped me to get a bank loan, but I only managed to buy more trouble. I went to a used-car lot, bought a van for $3,800, and drove it off the lot at 5:45 p.m. to go directly to work because my shift started at six p.m. After work, I didn't even make it home before the van broke down, so I had to walk home and have the van towed to the garage where the mechanic told me it needed two thousand dollars in repairs. I was so depressed that I did not eat for two days. I did not go to work or school—I just lay in bed, worrying about the loan. All I could do was pray. I begged God to show me how I could overcome all the difficulties facing me in America.

After that low point, my prayers were answered. God gave me the strength to go back to work and school because we needed to survive, and a short time later, one of the LSS volunteers came to my apartment and asked me come with her. As we walked to her car, she handed me the keys and asked me to drive. I was already in the traffic when she told me that the car was mine. I was so surprised that I stepped on the gas pedal instead of the brake, and I almost caused an accident. My body was shaking, and I could not stop the tears from coming. I thanked God for answering my prayers before I even thanked the woman.

A few days later, I met Pastor Rick of the Methodist church in Fargo. As we became acquainted, I told him of my car troubles and answered prayers. He joked that he, too, had a car for me, but I would have to pay one dollar for it. The Lord showed me that I will never have to worry about car problems again because he will provide a Christian car dealer—Pastor Rick!

I was so happy with my new car that I made the mistake of sending a package to my friends who still live in the camp in Kenya. I described my new life, and I sent some money, a pair of shoes, and some photographs. They did not rejoice with me, but they became bitter and told me that God does not love them because He has not given them a new life. They resented my happiness.

Since I came to North Dakota, I have adjusted to many aspects of life, but the winter is still a big problem for me. I am used to very hot temperatures, so I put on many layers of clothing to keep warm. One spring day I met one of my classmates in a store, but he did not recognize me because I looked so thin. He asked me if I had a twin brother at NDSU because he had seen someone just like me, only bigger. I explained that I wear four pairs of pants and two big jackets during the winter, so I look fat when the cold weather comes.

Looking back, I now realize how many misconceptions I had when I lived in Africa. I had thought that we, the Lost Boys of Sudan, were the only people with true faith in God. In each country, people gathered to watch us worship, dance, and sing gospel songs in our dialects because it was beautiful to watch. During our times of hardship, we prayed and expected miracles to happen, and they did. Now I know that America, too, has many Christians who preach the Word of God, who worship and pray in church, who sing in their choirs, and who give generously to others. I believe God purposely allowed us to experience severe suffering and brought us to this great Christian nation because he wants to prepare us to somehow help those we left behind in our country—the animists, the Christians in southern Sudan, and the black Muslims in Darfur who are suffering under Arab persecution. I believe it was the will of God that we should learn to read and write and gain access to the outside world so that we can understand and spread the Word of God.

I am particularly interested in helping the Christians who stayed behind in Sudan. During the civil war in the 1980s, Christians prayed that God would bring peace to their land so they could worship Him in freedom from Arab oppression. A common prayer was "Oh, God, we need our land, and it has become a land of birds of flesh, but not our land anymore! Oh, God, expel the evil and birds of flesh from our land by bringing peace!" The Episcopal church gained over three million converts in Sudan, and over five thousand men became pastors without any formal education. Nathanial Garang Anyiith became the bishop to oversee the spread of the gospel and the churches throughout the entire area.

I belong to a group that believes we should open a hospital in Darfur because the Muslims there are currently facing genocide from the northern government and suffering the results of war like we had in the south. On January 9, 2005, the twenty-one-year civil war in southern Sudan was ended when international leaders, including US Secretary of State Colin Powell and U.N. Ambassador John Danforth, witnessed the signing of a peace treaty between the Christians in the south and the Muslims in the north. Danforth and the U.N. Security Council had pressured both parties to sign an agreement, and the event was celebrated by southern Sudanese throughout the world, at home, and in exile—with many calling it an act of God.

Southern Sudan now lives in peace, so a Lost Boys Memorial Hospital could serve the war-torn Darfur area and set a godly example that the Lost Boys are behind them, even though they are Muslims. Our example might encourage the world leaders to, once again, stop the fighting and bring peace.

I do not know exactly what the future holds for me and my family, but I trust that God will continue to guide and protect us as He did in Sudan, Ethiopia, and Kenya. My Christian faith has been tested and strengthened by the journeys through the deserts of my life, so I am ready to continue my journey in America with courage and joy.